Sixty Years Ago; or, Reminiscences of the Struggle for the Freedom of the Press in South Africa, and the Establishment of the First Newspaper in the Eastern Province

SIXTY YEARS AGO;

OR,

REMINISCENCES

OF THE

Struggle for the Freedom of the Press

IN

SOUTH AFRICA,

AND THE

ESTABLISHMENT OF THE FIRST NEWSPAPER IN THE EASTERN PROVINCE.

BY

THE HON'BLE L. H. MEURANT,

MEMBER OF THE LEGISLATIVE COUNCIL.

CAPE TOWN:

SAUL SOLOMON & Co., PRINTERS, ST. GEORGE'S STREET.

1885.

DEDICATION.

TO THE

CHAIRMAN AND MEMBERS

OF THE

" Newspaper Press Union of South Africa "

The Reminiscences which the following pages contain are respectfully
Dedicated, by a Brother Pressman, the Senior in the Colony,
and the only person, he believes, now living, who has a
personal knowledge of many of the facts.

No fine writing has been attempted, the aim of the author having been to
place upon record as succinct and consecutive a history of the great
and successful struggle for the LIBERTY OF THE PRESS IN
SOUTH AFRICA, as is obtainable from published records
and other sources of information ; as well as of the
subsequent spread of Colonial Newspaper
Literature, especially in the Eastern
Province.

In the hope that what he has compiled and written may clear up several
controversial questions, and afford useful information, he now
submits the following pages to his Brother Pressmen
and the Public.

L. H. MEURANT.

Cape Town, May 30, 1885.

A 2

REMINISCENCES, &c.

"The mass of every People must be barbarous where there is no Printing."—*Johnson.*

Such was the sentiment, or motto, with which the first number of the *South African Commercial Advertiser* was ushered into life just sixty years ago, on the 7th January, 1824.

It has often been subject of thought, and matter of surprise, to the writer of these "Reminiscences," and others, that so long a period as between the first colonization of the Cape of Good Hope and the year 1824 was allowed to elapse without any attempt being made to establish a free public newspaper, or as it is now called a "Free Press," in this Colony.

This is the more surprising when we consider that the first Settlers came from what has been called "the most industrious and liberty-loving of countries—Holland,"—followed not very long after by the exiled Huguenots, "some of the best blood of La belle France."

To account for such supineness, or lack of energy, or whatever else it may be called, we must look to the state of Society immediately before, and at the period to which these Reminiscences refer ; and we find a remarkable coincidence of despotism, as will be seen hereafter, between the rule of the two nationalities—Dutch and English. For nearly a century and a half the Cape of Good Hope was a mere mercantile settlement of the Dutch East India Company, who held a monopoly of trade, and checked nnd prevented the formation of what is now understood as a Colony. The greed of self-aggrandizement was such that the Settlers were compelled to sell their produce exclusively to the " Company," at its own price, not being a tithe of its real value. It is a strange fact, that at the very period the States of Holland were distinguished for the maintenance of public liberty and the encouragement of industry, their representatives at the new Colony of the Cape of Good Hope carried out a policy directly the reverse. The French refugees had also on oath promised compliance with the local regulations of the Company, which stipulated that no one in the Colony might sell the produce of their labour on their own terms—that neither could they buy nor dispose of anything except at the Company's store, and at the Company's price!

Among those early settlers there were several who; having some knowledge of personal right and freedom, were not likely to submit to the arbitrary rule of the Company without remonstrance ; thus we find that political and other troubles arose. The Governor (Willem Adriaan van der Stell—1699) and his father (Simon van der Stell) and his brother, were the largest farmers in the Colony, and the clergyman of Cape Town was the next greatest ; having, it was alleged, the slaves and property of the Company at command, and, being secure from interference, doing just as they pleased.

A memorial, signed by sixty-one of the Burghers, was, however, secretly forwarded to Holland, charging the Governor with personal persecution and tyranny, and with monopolizing every means of private profit.

When the Governor (W. A. van der Stell) discovered that such a memorial had left the Colony, he at once—like Lord Charles Somerset afterwards, under English rule—took proceedings against all who were known to have signed it. Among them we find the names recorded of several "refugees," such as Jacques de Savoye ; his son-in-law, named Meyer; Guilliam and François du Toit; Hercules du Pré; Cornelis van

Niekerk; Jacobus van Brakel; Willem van Zyl; Jan and
Carl Elbertz, and others—names still well-known at the
present day.

Such is a slight outline of the history of the time, ending
in the recall of Governor Van der Stell, but effecting no change
whatever in the policy of the Company, which, as before observed,
was self-aggrandizement. And this reference to it has been
here introduced to show how remarkably history repeated itself,
in many respects, in the subsequent despotic rule of the Anglo-
Colonial Government, upwards of a century afterwards.

The growth of the Cape of Good Hope, it may be truly
said, as a free Colony—properly so called—dates from the
arrival of the first British Immigration in 1820. This was
the largest influx in a body of really " free " people since the
first settlement of the Colony, and this fact must be borne in.
mind, as having a direct influence upon the subsequent attempt
to establish a *Free Press*. Prior to that date, the only acces-
sions from the United Kingdom were a few merchants and
traders, and the civil and military officers appointed to the
Station.

The "Zuurveldt"—now the district of Albany—had previously been occupied by the T"Slambie Kafirs, who were
intruders—the Colonial boundaries being then the Fish River,
from its source to the sea;—they were driven out by a mixed
Imperial and Colonial force, under command of the late Colonel
Graham, after whom Graham's Town has been named. This
fine vacated country had to be filled up. The time was oppor-
tune. The war with Napoleon the First had stagnated trade,
and emigration was looked to as an outlet for the relief of the
unemployed. The introduction of emigrants to fill up the
Zuurveldt was recommended to the Home authorities; the
suggestion found favour, and £50,000 was voted by the British
Parliament for the purpose. No less than 90,000 applications
were sent in, although only about 4,000 persons could be sent

out for the money. Eventually 3,475 souls were landed in Algoa Bay (Port Elizabeth) in April, 1820.

Amongst the Settlers thus introduced were many men of good position and education, several of whom played conspicuous parts subsequently in Cape public affairs. There were four practical printers, viz., the late Hon'bles R. Godlonton and William Cock ; Thos. Stringfellow (subsequently Civil Commissioner and Resident Magistrate of Fort Beaufort), and Samuel Mollett (afterwards overseer in the printing office of Mr. W. Bridekirk, proprietor of the *South African Chronicle*, Cape Town). Then there were the late Hon'ble J. C. Chase, Capt. Duncan Campbell (late Civil Commissioner of Albany), Lieut. T. C. White (murdered by Kafirs in the war of 1834-35), Lieut. Rubidge, R.N., Walter Currie (father of the late Sir Walter, then one year old), Dr. John Atherstone (father of the Hon. W. G. Atherstone, then five years old), George Dyason (afterwards Civil Commissioner of Graaff-Reinet), Hougham Hudson (afterwards Civil Commissioner and Resident Magistrate of Graham's Town, father of the present Civil Commissioners of Graaff-Reinet and Oudtshoorn), Revs. Shaw, Boardman and McCleland, Lieut. Bisset, R N. (father of Lieut.-General Sir J. J. Bisset), Miles Bowker, with his nine sons (father of the Hon'ble R. M. Bowker), the Thornhills, Carlisles, Gilfillans, Lovemores, Scanlens (grandfather and father of Sir Thomas), Capt. Damant, Alexander Biggar (and his seven daughters) and son Robert, who was killed in a fight at Blood River, Zululand, many years ago, Dr. Roberts, Dr. Peter Campbell, Dr. John Younger, Thomas Phillips, David and Carey Hobson, the Cawoods, Thomas Mahoney (murdered by Kafirs in the Kafir invasion of 1834), George Southey, with his sons William, Richard (the Honourable), George and Henry : and last, though not least, Thomas Pringle, who subsequently fought the battle of the Liberty of the South African Press. With an influx of such men it will not be surprising that there was a shaking among the dry bones.

On the arrival of the British Settlers, the Colony was governed by the Acting Governor, Sir Rufane Shawe Donkin, "who earned for himself the gratitude of the whole Settlement by the sympathy he showed for the misfortunes of the Settlers, and by his efforts to ameliorate their condition." Great were the hardships and privations of the Settlers. Two successive years their crops failed, and the distress from this and other misfortunes became so great that the English Government had to spend no less a sum than £200,000 to meet the demands for rations, agricultural implements, &c.

On the 1st of December, 1821, Lord Charles Henry Somerset, the Governor (who had been absent on leave), returned to the Colony. He was a despot in every sense of the word, and the British Settlers, coming so recently from a free country, soon became sensible of the want of a Free Press, and felt the paralyzing oppressiveness of absolute despotism. The late Mr. John Fairbairn, in his preface to a "condensed edition of the first eighteen numbers of the *South African Commercial Advertiser*," published in 1826, thus describes the rule of Lord Charles :—"The slightest expression of discontent was considered by those who knew the Colony as an act of great imprudence, exposing the obnoxious individual to the whole force of Government opposition in all his pursuits. Formal complaints, however just and reasonable, were met with neglect, or insult, or with punishments of a more substantial nature, the Colony being in so artificial a state that the higher powers could ruin almost any man, merely by withdrawing its favour from him, while it was bestowed upon his rival; thus destroying the balance between them." "Neither character nor talent was proof against the proud man's contumely, or the insolence of office."

Previous to the arrival of the British Settlers in 1820,

this tyrannical and vindictive system met with little or weak resistance on the part of the public. The British Settlers were the first to represent to Earl Bathurst (then Secretary of State for the Colonies) by memorial, in 1823, their complaints against the system of government and laws to which they were subject. This petition was laid on the table of the House of Commons, the result being that a Commission of Inquiry was appointed to investigate the affairs of the Settlement on the spot.

What precipitated this action on the part of the British Settlers was the publication in the *Government Gazette*—the only paper then printed in the Colony, a paper entirely under the control of the Government, not even an advertisement being admitted without its sanction—of the following

"PROCLAMATION

"Of His Excellency the Right Honourable Lord CHARLES HENRY SOMERSET, &c , &c.

"Whereas it has been represented to me that certain individuals (probably ignorant of the laws of the Colony) have proposed to convene public meetings for the discussion of public measures and political subjects, contrary to the law and usage of this place, I deem it, therefore, necessary thus publicly to notify that all meetings so convened are contrary to law, and that every person who attempts to convene any meeting or assembly of such nature, without my sanction and authority, or the authority of the Chief Local Magistrate, in distant districts when the object of such meeting may be of so urgent a nature, that my authority and sanction cannot be obtained, or any person *attending* such unsanctioned meetings, is guilty of a high misdemeanour, and is severely punishable for such offence : And I, moreover, hereby warn all persons who may, notwithstanding, be induced to convene, or attend, any such public meeting, that the local authorities have been authorized and required to disperse the same ; and after the promulgation of these presents, to arrest and bring to justice all and every individual who shall infringe the *ancient Laws* and Usages of the Colony entrusted to my care.

" And whereas certain ignorant, malevolent, or designing persons have thought proper to assert and insinuate that the Governor of this Colony is not duly made acquainted with the petitions or complaints preferred by those who feel themselves aggrieved, or who have occasion to address me, as His Majesty's Representative, on their respective cases and interests, I do therefore deem it advisable to acquaint all persons that in no instance is any petition, memorial or letter addressed to this Government, which does not come under my immediate cognizance, or in which the order is not given under my own hand, and that in most instances the contrary supposition is alone adduced to cover language and expressions which could not be tolerated if addressed immediately to His Majesty's Representative, without offence to the laws in this case provided.

" And I do hereby further make known that, participating most anxiously and sincerely in the distress which has been unavoidably felt, from the total failure of two successive harvests, and various other causes, by such of my countrymen as sought an asylum in this Settlement in the year 1820, I shall unceasingly court every opportunity of reducing their real grievances, and of promoting their general and individual welfare; but that it is at the same time my firm determination to put down, by all the means with which the law has entrusted me, such attempts as have been recently made to disturb the public peace, whether by inflammatory or libellous writings, or by any other measures, of which I give those concerned this public warning, that no one may have cause to plead ignorance of the laws of the Colony, when called to account for transactions so materially and injuriously affecting the public peace.

GOD SAVE THE KING !

" Given under my hand and seal, at the Cape of Good Hope, this 24th day of May, 1822.

" (Signed)   C. H. SOMERSET.

" By His Excellency's Command,

" (Signed)   C. BIRD, Secretary."

Another act of despotism against the Settlers was, that a certain Colonel Jones, Chief Magistrate of Albany, who had been appointed by Sir Rufane Donkin, and who had become popular with the Settlers, was summarily dismissed from office, from personal pique of the Governor, it was alleged, and the seat of Magistracy, which up to that date had been at Bathurst, was removed to Graham's Town, causing very considerable loss to many of the inhabitants of the former place ; in fact ruining it altogether. Capt. Duncan Campbell and Mr. Miles Bowker (before referred to), who had been associated with Colonel Jones as Heemraden, or Assessors, resigned their appointments, refusing to serve any longer under such a Government.

Mr. Thomas Pringle, the able writer and sweet poet, head of the Scotch party of Settlers, located on the Baviaan's River (now Glen Lynden), had in the meantime found his way to Cape Town, where, through the influence of his countryman, Sir Walter Scott, with the home Government, he obtained the post of sub-librarian to the South African Public Library. " For some time after my arrival in Cape Town," wrote Mr. Pringle, " things appeared to wear a favourable aspect. The Governor had declared himself a friend to the mitigation of Slavery, and had just issued a Proclamation containing some beneficial and many plausible enactments " . . . " While matters exhibited this encouraging aspect, and while I saw opening around me fields of public usefulness, far beyond my own humble powers adequately to occupy, I wrote home to invite Mr. Fairbairn, an early and intimate friend, to join me at Cape Town, in order to share with me in the toils, and (as I then hoped) the honours of the career I had too sanguinely sketched out for our joint activity."

Mr. Fairbairn having in due course joined his friend Pringle, the latter says :—" Long before Mr. Fairbairn joined me, however, I had acquired a more intimate acquaintance with the character of the Colonial Administration, and formed a truer estimate of their views. I soon saw that their professed anxiety to encourage education and the diffusion of knowledge, was but a piece of political hypocrisy, assumed to cloak the real character of the Government from the prying eyes of His Majesty's Commissioners of Inquiry, whose arrival in the Colony was then daily expected."*

A remarkable combination of circumstances appeared to favour the advent of a *Free Press*. As already stated Mr. Thomas Pringle had taken up his residence in Cape Town, where he was soon joined by Mr. John Fairbairn. At this very time Mr. George Greig, a gentleman who had held an appointment in the King's Printing Office in London—a practical printer—arrived in the Colony, bringing with him the necessary plant for a printing establishment. Almost at the same time a vessel arrived in Table Bay on her way to India, having on board a quantity of new printing type destined for a periodical in India, but which had suddenly ceased to exist, and instructions had been received in Cape Town to sell the type if possible. The writer's father, having become acquainted with Mr. Greig, and being equally anxious with others to see a Free Press established in the Colony, purchased the type for Mr. Greig, for the sum of £300, on the understanding with the latter that his only son (the writer) should be taught the art of printing, and when sufficiently old should be admitted a partner in the business.

One of the aims of Mr. Pringle was to establish an independent periodical in Cape Town; and he soon found a zealous coadjutor in the late Rev. Dr. Abraham Faure, who also wished to start a Dutch periodical. The former, in which Mr. Fairbairn was to take part, was to be called the *South African Journal*, the latter *De Zuid Afrikaansche Tydschrift*, being the same

---

* Appointed in consequence of the memorial of the British Settlers.

signification in Dutch. On the 23rd February, 1823, Messrs. Pringle and Faure sent a joint memorial to the Governor, requesting *permission* for their works, and received a *verbal* reply, through the lips of the Colonial Secretary—"His Excellency the Governor has not seen your application in a favourable light."

Mr. Pringle suggested to write again, from which course he was dissuaded by the Colonial Secretary (as a private friend). "The Governor's jealousy of an independent Press," said the Colonial Secretary, "was too deep-rooted to be influenced by any force of argument, and to demand a written reply would be regarded as a most offensive proceeding." So the matter dropped for the present.

The Commission of Inquiry—Mr. Bigge and Mr. Cole-brooke—arrived in July following.

"While matters were in this position," says Mr. Pringle, " I was surprised on the 2nd December, by a summons from the Governor, to receive a communication on the subject of the Press. His Excellency informed me that Earl Bathurst had been pleased to permit the publication of our proposed journal, provided care was taken that nothing appeared in it 'detrimental to the peace and safety of the Colony.' After some admonitory remarks of his own, Lord Charles gave, with obvious reluctance, and with a very ill grace, his sanction for us to proceed with the publication."

Previous to this interview, in July, 1823, Mr. Greig sent the following memorial to the Governor, it being understood that such a course was necessary :—

"To His Excellency Lord CHARLES HENRY SOMERSET, Governor of His Majesty's Settlement of the Cape of Good Hope.

" HUMBLY SHEWETH,—

" That your memorialist is by profession a printer and stationer, and a Freeman of the Stationers' Company.

" That your memorialist for several years held a situation in His Majesty's Printing Office in London, which, owing to some new arrangements in that department, and other causes, he thought fit to relinquish,—receiving at the same time from the hands of that department testimonials honourable to his conduct and professional talents, which he has in his possession.

" That your memorialist embarked a considerable capital in the purchase of materials used in the printing and stationery business, with a view of following his profession in this Colony, and your memorialist is therefore anxious to obtain your Excellency's approbation in attempting to establish himself in a profession to which he has devoted his early years, and the relinquishment of which must subject him to a very serious pecuniary loss. In prosecution of these views your memorialist is desirous of commencing a publication, which will combine the ordinary topics of a magazine, and more particularly such as are interesting to the commercial and agricultural parts of the community, but rigidly excluding *personal* controversy, and all discussion of matter relating to the policy or administration of the Colonial Government.

" That your memorialist not only finds the commercial body of the Colony generally favourable to the above project, but has the satisfaction of being zealously supported in his views by many, who consider it highly important to their welfare and interests, that an established record of this nature should exist to circulate authentic information in regard to current circumstances, and as a work of after reference. In regard to the other objects of the work, your memorialist deems it unnecessary to point out the advantages at all times derived from a free diffusion of knowledge, it being indisputable that in proportion as just and liberal sentiments prevail in any community, the public character becomes more elevated, and the influence of Religion and Morality more deep and lasting. In support of this assertion your memorialist begs to refer to the colony of New South Wales—where, since the establishment of a newspaper and magazine, a new and higher tone has been given to Society—more liberality prevails between the different classes—men of literary acquirements devote their talent to the advancement of the general good—ideas have been suggested from which the most important results are daily accruing—the cause of virtue and religion is advocated in an agreeable and instructive manner, and vice and licentiousness is held up to detestation, in language powerfully convincing, yet free from anything to which the most scrupulous decorum could object ; in short, the whole Colony is advanced in comfort, its commerce greatly improved, and its Government less fettered.

"Your memorialist is well aware that in the event of your Excellency granting your sanction to the establishment of a Printing Press, and the publication of a " Literary and Commercial Magazine," there are various individuals of literary talent in this Colony who will be ready to afford their zealous support to this enterprise, in the view of contributing to the general improvement of the Colony, not only as respects its commerce and agriculture, but also in the still more important departments of Education, Morality and Religion. Your Excellency's anxious desire to promote these important objects cannot be doubted. Your memorialist only prays, therefore, that you may be pleased to view his design as calculated to produce so desirable a result, while at the same time the restrictions he has suggested in the plan will obviate all danger of its ever conflicting in any point with the political system of the Colony.

" In conclusion, your memorialist begs to express his readiness (if required for your Excellency's satisfaction) to produce certificates of his capability in every respect of properly conducting the projected work, which he now respectfully submits to your Excellency's consideration, humbly, yet confidently, anticipating from your candour and justice a favourable determination.

" And your memorialist, as in duty bound, will ever pray.

"(Signed)   GEORGE GREIG.

"Cape Town, July, 1823."

If a thunderbolt had fallen at the feet of the despotic Governor it could not have produced greater consternation at Government House. Indeed, such a memorial, to such a man appears the most refined sarcasm. His Excellency was in no hurry to send a reply. About a month was allowed to elapse in concocting some feasible excuse for a negative answer, when on the 14th August, 1823, the following official letter was received by Mr. Greig, and from that day "The Battle of the Freedom of the Press" commenced :—

"REPLY to the Memorial of Mr. GEORGE GREIG, by profession a Printer and Stationer, praying His Excellency the Governor's sanction to the establishment of a Printing Press, and the publication of a 'Literary and Commercial Magazine.'

"Memorialist is informed that His Excellency the Governor having had *numerous applications* to the same purport as that of memorialist, His Excellency will feel himself bound to consider the interests of prior applicants whenever a Printing Press shall be established in the Colony.

"By command of His Excellency,

"(Signed)   C. BIRD.

"Colonial Office, August 14, 1823."

The reason assigned for the refusal was a subterfuge. With the exception of the subsequent application of Messrs. Pringle and Faure, no similar application had ever been made—especially from a Printer (it being understood that the works of Messrs. Pringle and Faure were to be printed at the Government Printing Establishment). The only other instance on record regarding a printing office being, that when one of the Settlers ships, the *Chapman*, put into Table Bay three years previously, there were on board Messrs. Godlonton and Stringfellow, who brought with them the whole plant of a printing establishment, destined for Albany. But they were not permitted to take it on, the Government, in the most despotic manner, seizing, or as it would now be termed, "jumping" the whole, and paying the invoice price. This press and those printing materials afterwards, strange to say, fell into the hands of the writer, and subsequently came into the

B

possession of one of the original proprietors, Mr. Godlonton, as will be seen in the sequel.

The "numerous applications" was a myth. It appears almost incredible, at the present day, that a British Governor, a scion of one of the noblest houses in Great Britain, would, in order to carry out his despotic designs, descend to actual untruth, or something very like it.

Messrs. Pringle and Fairbairn had opened an academy, which found great favour with the inhabitants, and was in a most flourishing condition. On the 5th March, 1824, they printed the first number of their *Magazine* at the Government printing establishment, which was warmly welcomed by a respectable body of subscribers. "No objection," says Mr. Pringle, "was openly made to any expression in the first number of our magazine; though I afterwards learnt that several articles had given umbrage to the Governor and his confidential advisers. The second number of Mr. Pringle's magazine appeared on the 7th May. On the 13th the Fiscal sent Mr. Pringle a summons to attend at his office, where he informed him (Pringle) that several articles and paragraphs in the magazine had given high offence to the Government; that had the obnoxious passages been observed while the work was in the press, he (the Fiscal) would have expunged them, or suppressed the number; that he must now have a satisfactory pledge, that nothing ' obnoxious ' or offensive to Government should appear in future." The result, after a long conversation, was, that on the following day Messrs. Fairbairn and Pringle sent the Fiscal a written notice to the effect that the magazine would be discontinued, rather than submit to the "Censorship" of the Fiscal.

Shortly before these events—for they took place in quick succession—Mr. Greig, being disappointed by the answer of the Governor to his memorial, adopted an independent course. Having made inquiries, and finding there was *no law*

in existence hostile to the publication in this Colony of such a
work as he had projected, he resolved to start a newspaper instead
of a magazine. Accordingly, on the 30th December, 1823,
he published the following

"PROSPECTUS

"OF THE 'SOUTH AFRICAN COMMERCIAL ADVERTISER.'

"The *South African Commercial Advertiser* is intended chiefly for
the use and accommodation of persons connected with trade and
merchandise. Its columns will be open for advertisements, at a
reasonable charge, in the English and Dutch languages, announcing
sales, arrivals of goods, and such other matters as the merchant or
retail dealer may wish to make known ; also rates of exchange,
arrivals and departures of vessels, state of the markets, and any
information that may tend to the advancement of trade and commerce, the improvement of agriculture, or the elucidation of
science.

"A small portion of the *South African Commercial Advertiser* will
be appropriated to original miscellaneous matter, in which will be discussed subjects at once interesting and amusing. Occasional extracts
will be made from English papers and other literary productions ; an
offering to the muses ; or an inoffensive point of humour may find
room in its columns. And while we shall be happy to receive
communications from intelligent correspondents, the *South African
Commercial Advertiser* will ever most rigidly exclude all personal
controversy, however disguised, or the remotest discussion of
subjects relating to the policy or administration of the Colonial
Government.

"As we are desirous of obtaining the earliest information tending
to improvements in agriculture, we shall be happy to receive
communications from persons acquainted with this branch of
science.

"In submitting to the public a prospectus of the *South African
Commercial Advertiser* we are aware of the difficulties that must in
its outset attend an enterprise of this nature. Our promises,
therefore, respecting literature must be, for the present, limited.

To those whose talents have hitherto lain dormant for want of an opportunity of exerting them, a facility is now offered, which we hope will develop genius, and raise the literary reputation of the Colony ; and as a free diffusion of knowledge is the grand means of giving a tone to Society, by elevating its morals, and promoting a taste for literature, we look to the more enlightened part of the community, in the confident hope that they will not allow this, the first, attempt to establish a medium of general communication in a British Colony to fall for want of that support which the well-informed, the intelligent, and the patriotic are alone able to afford." [Here follows a list of the terms, days of publication, &c.]

A copy of this prospectus, accompanied with the following note, was sent to the Governor :—

"My Lord,—I have the honour to enclose for your Lordship's perusal a prospectus of the *South African Commercial Advertiser*. I am induced to calculate on your Lordship's Patronage from a conviction that the utility of such a medium of general communication cannot fail to be obvious to your Excellency ; while at the same time its mild and harmless plan will obviate all doubts as to its tendency. Independent of these grounds, I feel assured it cannot be your Excellency's object to raise any barrier against my following a profession which (from having studied it) I have full right to look up to for support.

"I have the honour, &c,

"(Signed)   George Greig.

"December 20, 1823."

This clever "feeler," and introduction of the thin edge of the wedge, did not evoke any reply, and accordingly on Wednesday, the 7th January, 1824, the first number of the *South African Commercial Advertiser*—the first free newspaper printed since the formation of the Colony in 1652 – made its appearance at what was then No. 1, Longmarket-street, opposite Caledon-square, on the premises then occupied by Mr. George Luck (ominous name) as a wine store. And here, for such an auspicious event, it may be permitted—considering the times and the difficulties attendant on the work, mechanical as well as literary—to record the names of those engaged upon it:—George Greig, editor and proprietor; compositors, &c, Michael Kearns, John Eckley, Louis Henri Meurant—the latter the only one now left to tell the tale.

Great was the sensation in Cape Town on the morning of publication. For hours previously the street was thronged with people, and so great was the demand that a large extra number of copies had to be printed.

It is not surprising that after what had already taken place every subsequent number of the *South African Commercial Advertiser* was closely scrutinized. Mr. Pringle states:—"It was the *newspaper* which they (the Government) regarded with the deepest dislike, and which they watched with unsleeping vigilance for an opportunity to pounce upon and crush it. We had introduced the practice of reporting law cases, and on this point the Governor and some of his advisers happened to be peculiarly sensitive, insomuch that although they had nothing to allege against the paper as respects the impartiality and discretion with which such reports had been given, they could not tolerate the continuance of such a privilege."

Return we now to the *South African Journal.* "The Cape Reign of Terror," says Pringle, "had now commenced; and events succeeded each other with a rapidity and violence which the actors mistook for energy and decision." The second number of the *Magazine* had been published on the 7th May. After the interview between the Fiscal and Mr. Pringle, on the 13th, and after the written notice of Messrs. Fairbairn and Pringle to the Fiscal on the 15th, Pringle was sent for by the Governor, to appear immediately before him at his audience room in the Colonial Office. "I found him," says Mr. Pringle, "with the Chief Justice, Sir John Truter, seated on his right hand, and the second number of our *South African*

Journal lying open before him. There was a storm on his brow, and it burst forth at once upon me like a long-gathered south-easter from Table Mountain. 'So, Sir,' he began, 'you are one of those who dare to insult me and oppose my government,' and then he launched forth in a long tirade of abuse; scolding, upbraiding and taunting me, with all the domineering arrogance of mien and sneering insolence of expression of which he was so great a master, reproaching me above all for my *ingratitude* for his personal favours. While he thus addressed me, in the most insulting style, I felt my frame tremble with indignation; but I saw that the Chief Justice was placed there for a witness of my demeanour, and that my destruction was sealed if I gave way to my feelings, and was not wary in my words. I stood up, however, and confronted this most arrogant man with a look under which his haughty eye instantly sunk, and replied to him with a calmness of which I had not, a few minutes before, thought myself capable. I told him I was quite sensible of the position in which I stood—a very humble individual before the Representative of my Sovereign; but I also knew what was due to myself as a British subject and a gentleman, and that I would not submit to be *rated* in the style he had assumed by any man, whatever even his station or rank. I repelled his charges of having acted unworthily of my character as a Government servant and a loyal subject; I defended my conduct in regard to the Press, and the character of our *Magazine*, which he said was full of 'calumny and falsehood'; I asserted my right to petition the King *for the extension of the Freedom of the Press* in the Colony; and I denied altogether the 'personal obligations' with which he upbraided me, having never asked, nor received from him, the slightest personal favour, unless the lands allotted to my party, and my own appointment to the Government library, were considered such, though the latter was, in fact, a public duty assigned to me, in compliance with the recommendations of the Home Government. This situation, however, I now begged to resign, since I would not compromise my free agency for that or any appointment his Lordship could bestow."

This bold front of Mr. Pringle appeared to have staggered the despot and bully, who " immediately lowered his tone, and had the singular meanness, after the insulting terms he had used," to attempt a coaxing tone, and repeatedly invited Mr. Pringle to recommence the *Magazine,* which the latter declined unless *legal protection* were granted to the Press.

It will be necessary here to make a slight digression, to give a few pictures of the state of Cape Town at the period referred to in these Reminiscences. The Commissioners of Inquiry, before referred to, had arrived in the Colony in July, 1823. A " Free Press " was the most inopportune event that could possibly happen. A great trial—in which Lord Charles Somerset was deeply and personally interested—was to come off almost immediately after the establishment of Mr. Greig's Free newspaper, and the proceedings would be reported. To crush the paper, which had been started in spite of the Governor, and thus stifle the expression of public opinion, now became the paramount object. The Supreme Court of Justice (*Raad van Justicie*) was then differently constituted to what it is now, and the mode of proceeding would hardly be recognized now-a-days. When the Chief Justice submitted to be rated, and bullied, and intimidated by the Governor—as will be seen hereafter—it could hardly be expected that there would be much impartiality amongst its members The Court consisted of eight Judges, or members (Leden), with a Chief Justice at its head. Cases were generally tried by two " Commissioners " (members) of the Court, excepting in cases of appeal, when the full Court, with the Chief Justice, sat ; there being also a final appeal to the Governor himself. The officers of the Court consisted of a Fiscal—tantamount to the present Attorney-General or Public Prosecutor—and some minor officials, such as the *Bode* (Sheriff), &c. The office of Fiscal was held by Mr. Daniel Denyssen (father of the late esteemed Judge), a profound Dutch lawyer. This gentleman bore a foremost part in the subsequent proceedings with reference to the *South African Commercial Advertiser*, and also in what may be termed the State Trials, nominally instituted by the Fiscal, but virtually by the Governor, Lord Charles Somerset.

The reign of this Governor, at that period, as correctly stated by Mr. Thomas Pringle, was the " Reign of Terror." No public meeting, as has been shown, could be held without the Governor's consent. " The Governor's power was absolute, and his resentment ruin." It was difficult, indeed, to conjecture to what lengths the violence of arbitrary power would at that dismal period proceed. " A frightful system of *espionage* pervaded every circle of Society, and rendered perilous even the confidence of the domestic hearth." The fear of exposure appeared to infuriate the Governor, " who seemed determined to strike down every man who should dare even to *look* or *think* disapprobation of his deeds." *Oliver*, the well-known Government spy of the period (under an assumed name, and whom the writer well remembers), " who had been sent out from England to be provided for at the Cape with a lucrative situation under Lord Charles, was most actively engaged during this crisis, as was universally believed, in his former vocation. Informers and false witnesses (of whom the writer could mention many names) abounded; and rumours of ' plots ' and ' disloyal combinations against the Governor ' were assiduously kept afloat for purposes as obvious as they were mischievous.'*

*A " black-book " was kept at Government-house, in which appeared the names—assiduously reported by *Oliver* and his emissaries (many of whom the writer could name on indisputable authority, but for obvious reasons is suppressed)—in which was entered the names of all who were alleged to be " Liberals," Radicals, &c., and those destined for *immediate* destruction were designated by a X.

" The *Government Gazette* had been systematically employed for purposes of public deception, and sometimes of personal calumny. It had denounced the most respectable heads of the Albany Settlers as seditious Radicals, merely becaure they proposed to meet to petition the Government respecting their grievances." " The state of Society in Cape Town, and indeed throughout the Colony, at this period was truly deplorable. Mutual confidence was shaken ; distrust, apprehension and gloom everywhere prevailed ; and men, according to their several characters and circumstances, were perturbed by angry excitement or prostrated by slavish fear."*

These may appear overdrawn pictures, at this distance of time, *Sixty years ago*; but they are not so. The writer, although then still very young, but gifted with an excellent memory, can well remember the " Cape Reign of Terror," and vouch for the general accuracy of what has been here recorded.

But, *revenon a nos moutons.*—What is now Adderley-street was then called *Heerengracht* (gentleman's avenue, or walk). In the Heerengracht resided many of the Dutch aristocracy of the time (there was an " upper ten " then, or at all events they were regarded as such, which comes to the same thing) ; in or about the centre of the street was a wide and deep canal. fringed with fir-trees —affording cover to spies, &c.—and supplied with sluice-gates, which were shut down or opened, as occasion required, during dry weather or heavy rains. This canal is now covered over and the trees have been cut down. At one corner of Longmarket-street and Heerengracht stood a large house, the residence at one time of a Mr. Dreyer ; it had a huge rounded corner and very high " stoep," and was known as " Dreyer's Corner." At the opposite corner, opening into the Heerengracht, was the

* Pringle's Narrative of a Residence in South Africa.

late Mr. James Howell's Circulating Library and Stationer's shop; and a few doors further down towards the Bay, was the *African Society House*, a sort of club, where the officers of the Garrison and the *elite* of Cape Town used to assemble, discussing the topics of the day, &c. Howell's and Dreyer's corners were also places of public resort, especially the latter.*

The conductors of the *South African Commerical Advertiser* having studiously, and very properly, refrained from making the paper the medium of personal attacks, especially on the Government, " Dreyer's corner " during the excitement which prevailed in consequence of the "State Trials," was placarded almost every morning with squibs, and although the " Dienders "(policemen) were ever on the watch, or pretended to be, the authors of the placards could not be discovered. The writer of these Reminiscences, although a mere lad at the time, frequently copied some of the squibs, many of them being still fresh in his memory.

An innocent piece of original Poetry, which appeared in the first number of the *Commerical Advertiser*, gave great umbrage to the " powers that be," probably in consequence of the evident allusion, or supposed allusion, in the 7th verse,

---

* To further show the state of feeling at the time, especially against the Fiscal, who was supposed to be the principal adviser of the unpopular Governor, it appears that one of the officers of the garrison had taken mortal offence at something the Fiscal had said or done. The conse. quence was a challenge to fight a duel. The Fiscal, of course, could not accept ; when one morning there appeared a placard .posted against the round stoep of Dreyer's corner, quite a daily occurrence for political squibs :—" Lost, stolen, or strayed, a white-livered Dog, answering to the name of ' Dan.' Whoever will bring the said dog to the African Society House, with a rope round his neck, will be well rewarded.— N.B. This dog is of no use to any Sportsman, as he does not stand fire." Thus was public feeling excited against a public officer, for doing what he considered his duty.

to the "duel," and generally the publicity which *The Paper* was to give. Here are the verses :—

THE PAPER.

In gown and slippers loosely drest,
And breakfast brought, a welcome guest,
What is it gives the meal a zest ?

            The Paper.

When new-laid eggs the table grace,
And smoking rolls are in their place,
Say what enlivens ev'ry face ?

            The Paper.

In vain the urn is hissing hot,
In vain rich Hyson stores the pot,
If the vile newsman has forgot

            The Paper.

What is't attracts the optic pow'rs
Of Ensign gay, when fortune show'rs
Down prospects of a "step" in ours ?

            The Paper.

What is't can make the man of law
Neglect the deed or plead to draw
Ca. Sa.—Fi. Fa. Indictment, Flaw ?

            The Paper.

What is't can soothe his client's woe,
And make him quite forget John Doe,
Nor think on Mister Richard Roe ?

            The Paper.

What is't informs the country round
What's stol'n or stray'd, what's lost or found,
Who's born, and who's put under ground ?

            The Paper.

What tells you all that's done and said,
The fall of beer and rise of bread,
And what fair lady's brought to bed ?
                              The Paper.

What is't narrates full many a story
Of Mr. Speaker, Whig and Tory,
And heroes all agog for glory ?
                              The Paper.

What is it gives the price of stocks,
Of Poyais Loans, and patent locks,
And Cape wine at the London Docks ?
                              The Paper.

Abroad, at home, infirm or stout,
In health, or raving with the gout,
Who possibly can do without
                              The Paper ?

Its worth and merits then revere,
And since it now begins the year.
Forget not 'midst your Christmas cheer,
Nor think you e'er can buy too dear
                              The Paper.

That in such a state of Society as has been described partizanship was soon engendered, and that great efforts were made by Government spies and others intent upon Government "loaves and fishes," to bring odium on the brave men who were fighting the battle of "Liberty" and the "Freedom of the Press," will not surprise any one. There existed in those days what were termed "Sasaatje and Rice" houses, places where a favourite Dutch dish, called "sasaatjes," were served in the evenings to customers. One of these places especially, kept by a Mr. D— v. d. B——, was noted as a rendezvous for supposed Government employés. A soup-plate of "kerrie" (mullagatawny), two "sasaatjes" (diamond-shaped inch-sized pieces of mutton, curried, and about half-a-dozen stuck upon a bamboo . skewer, and then roasted upon a grid-iron), a few spoonfuls of dry-boiled Patna rice, and the half of a pint-bottle of Cape wine, were served for a kwartje (4½d. or a quarter of a Rixdollar, which was 1s. 6d.), a piece of stout blue-back paper money. Clean table-cloths, and everything in good style, and several tidy slave women as waitresses,—and punctually at a fixed hour in the evening, was the rule of the house. The customers, often to the number of twenty and more, all "Afrikanders"—several of the upper ten—sat down. The host then, with great solemnity, stood up, and recited, as a sort of counter-blast to Dreyer's corner : —

> " O Heere der heere !
> Wie zal hier in Afrika meer regeere ;
> Alle die uit Engeland zijn gebannen,°
> Worden hier groote mannen ;
> En ons arme Hollandsche gezellen,
> Kan men de ribben op het lijf al tellen.
> Met een schelling per dag moet men zich mee geneeren,
> En als je daar niet genoeg mee hebt, dan moet je naar
>   Wagenmakers Vallei passeeren,
> Naar oude Van Riet† de Sequester ;
> O heere, wilt ons toch verlossen,
> Van al die Engelsche ossen,
> En leidt ons toch naar wenschen,
> Ons arme Hollandsche Christemenschen, Amen."

This was also one of the squibs which had appeared on "Dreyer's corner," and copied by the writer, and retained in his memory ever since.

The second number of the *Commercial Advertiser* appeared in due course on Wednesday, the 14th January, 1824, but there was nothing in particular in it, excepting the following, which was not calculated to remove the uneasiness regarding

---

* Referring to the new arrivals, and the "Settlaars," a term of reproach.
† Mr. Van der Riet was "Sequester," or Administrator of Insolvency.

the probable success of the paper :—"Our Printing Office, on Wednesday last, exhibited a scene which our warmest hopes would scarcely have allowed us to expect. The crowd of applicants for our paper continued to throng until an advanced hour in the afternoon. We were gratefully surprised to see so many of the Native (Dutch) inhabitants of this colony amongst our supporters ; and the numerous inquiries which were made as to our intention in future of translating into the Dutch language the most interesting parts of our miscellaneous intelligence, convinces us of the expediency of making arrangements for that purpose ; but as this plan will require some time for completion, and will be attended with considerable expense, we trust that allowance will be made for the difficulties of our situation ; and that, in the meanwhile, our friends the Native inhabitants (Dutch) will continue their patronage and support."

Up to this period, neither Mr. Fairbairn nor Mr. Pringle had anything to do with the editorial part of the paper. With No. 3, on the 21st January, these gentlemen assumed the charge of the editorial department, writing in turns every alternate week.

A few days after the publication of the second number of the paper, Mr. Greig received the following letter : —

"Colonial Office, Jan. 28, 1824.

"Sir,—I am directed by His Excellency the Governor to inform you, that he has been pleased to fix the rate of postage to be paid for the paper you have established, at one skilling (2¼d.) for each number sent to the country.

"I am, &c.,

(Signed)   "P. G. Brink."

Here, then, was an official recognition of the *right* to establish and continue the issue of the *South African Commercial Advertiser*, a permission which the Governor had only a few weeks previously positively refused to grant. But there can be no doubt that the very able leading articles of the paper, after Messrs. Fairbairn and Pringle undertook the editorial management, without attacking the policy of the Government, but always keeping before the public the great boon of the *Liberty of the Press,* and extracts from celebrated authors on the same subject, tended to alarm the Government, and that a pretext was only wanting to extinguish the light which was gradually dawning upon the people, especially the " Native inhabitants" (Afrikanders).

Thus Mr. Pringle wrote :—" For a few months everything went on most prosperously. · The newspaper, which we published both in English and Dutch, was popular beyond our most sanguine expectations ; and our *Magazine,* of which the first number was issued on the 5th March, was also welcomed by a respectable body of subscribers. Our Academy was also in a very flourishing state, and the number of pupils constantly increasing." " In order to lessen, if possible, the morbid jealousy of the Governor, we printed our *Magazine* at the Government press, although the printing thus cost us more, and was far worse executed, than if we had consented to have had it done by Mr. Greig ; and we ventured to flatter. ourselves that the Colonial Authorities, in spite of their former habits, would, for their own credit, under the eyes of His Majesty's Commissioners, not venture really to interfere with us. But we were soon roughly awakened from our dream of security." " We had introduced the practice of reporting *Law Cases,* and on this point the Governor and some of his advisers happened to be peculiarly sensitive."

The immediate cause for the Governor's interference for the suppression of the paper, was this " sensitiveness" regarding the publication of Law Reports, especially of one in which he was personally and deeply concerned. There was a case then pending before the Supreme Court, at the instance of the Governor. A gentleman, named Launcelot Cook, had reported

a high official, Mr. Charles Blair, Collector of Customs —an
intimate friend of Lord Charles Somerset—to the Lords
Commissioners of His Majesty's Treasury, bringing very
serious charges of malversation against the said Mr. Blair, and
requesting inquiry. The memorial of Mr. Cook was dated
the 22nd January, 1824, and had been drawn up by a Mr.
William Edwards, a very able but reckless man, styling himself
an English lawyer. The memorial had been sent to the
Governor, but instead of being forwarded to England, or an
investigation ordered, it was detained by the Governor, and a
criminal action for libel instituted against Messrs. Cook and
Edwards, and a celebrated Dutch lawyer, Mr. Johan Bernhardt
Hoffman (better known by the sobriquet of "Scheele Hoffman").
The case came on for trial before two Commissioners of the
Court on the 16th Feb., 1824. Two days before this trial was
first heard in Cape Town, the Commissioners of Inquiry before
referred to arrived in Graham's Town. As the publication of the
trial in question appeared to be one of the principal reasons for
the arbitrary and high-handed proceeding of the Governor, in
order to suppress publicity, by stopping the paper, it is here
given very nearly *in extenso*. Reading the proceedings at this
distance of time, there can be very little doubt that not only the
Fiscal (Prosecutor) but the Court also, were inspired by the
Governor, who was virtually Prosecutor, Judge and Jury ; and
who would have had eventually to decide the case if finally heard
before himself in Appeal. Cape Town was in a state of great
excitement. The Court-room (the same now used in Cape
Town) was thronged with listeners. "Dreyer's Corner" was
plastered all over with placards The Fiscal had the best legal
talent in the Colony pitted against him,—Advocate (afterwards
Judge) Cloete, Advocate (afterwards Sir Christopher) Brand,
Mr. Edwards (a host in himself, whatever his character or
antecedents), and the wily and slim and most able Dutch
lawyer, Johan Bernhardt Hoffman, who will still be remem-

bered by many of the old hands in Cape Town.   It was THE *cause celebré* of the period :—

(From the " S. A. Commercial Advertiser," February 18, 1824.)

MONDAY, FEBRUARY 16TH, 1824.

Before W. BENTINCK and P. J. TRUTER, Esqrs., as Commissioners of the Court.

HIS MAJESTY'S FISCAL *vs.* LAUNCELOT COOK, WM. EDWARDS AND J. B. HOFFMAN.

This was an *ex-officio* prosecution brought by His Majesty's Fiscal against the defendants, charging the first with having written and signed, the second with having drawn up and forwarded to His Excellency the Governor, and the third with having copied, a certain libellous statement, in the shape of a Memorial to the Lords of the Treasury, accusing Mr. C. Blair, Collector of His Majesty's Customs, of having committed divers malpractices in the distribution of Prize Negroes, and of having in many instances made donations of these people to satisfy the claims of several of his creditors.   A list of about sixty witnesses (among whom the name of His Excellency the Governor appeared) was exhibited by His Majesty's Fiscal, as containing the names of witnesses required by the second defendant ; but to this mode of proceeding the Fiscal objected, as being contrary to the Roman Dutch Law, which leaves it to the discretion of the Judges to inquire into the nature of the evidence, and authorizes them to select those only who appear relevant to the matter at issue ; and, therefore, prayed that the Court should require from the defendants to state the facts to which they required every witness to speak, with liberty to the Judge to curtail such as might not be relevant.

The Court decreed the inquiry to be proceeded in regularly—reserving to themselves to decide upon this question after the *interrogatories* were answered by the defendants.

Upon proceeding to the interrogatories, the second defendant, W. Edwards, proposed four exceptions, as a plea in abatement.

c

1st. That His Majesty's Fiscal had committed a gross neglect of duty in not attending to the 23rd Article of the Crown Trials, which directs that all trials should be proceeded in within *eight* days from the decree of the summons in person ; whereas the decree was granted by the Court on the 5th instant, and the trial commenced only this day, the 16th ; which by no rule of arithmetic could be made to come within the time prescribed by the statute.

2nd. That His Majesty's Fiscal had been guilty of a dereliction of duty, by not summoning *all* the witnesses to appear this day ; none in fact had been summoned—and this also was contrary to the 38th Article of the Crown Trials.

3rd. That His Majesty's Fiscal had been guilty of a gross and detestable falsehood, in not religiously adhering to the truth, and the evidence before him, as prescribed in the 36th Article of the Crown Trials ; he stating that a Prize Negro, William Cousins, had been compelled by threats of Mr. C. Blair, to return into his service after the expiration of his 14 years apprenticeship ; whereas the memorial to the Lords of the Treasury, deemed libellous, did not warrant that assertion ; as nothing could have compelled that negro to return into his service.

The defendant (Mr. Edwards) was proceeding to charge His Majesty's Fiscal with similar untruths—which, in his opinion, would render him liable to corporal punishment—when the Fiscal arose and in great warmth claimed the protection of the Court against the scurrilous language used by the defendant. The Court, after having twice warned the defendant against using such indecorous language, condemned him to imprisonment for one month, and postponed the trial until a future day.[o]

[o] The imprisonment was most rigorously carried out. Mr. Edwards was confined in a cell in the old "Tronk" (Prison), then in "Rogge Bay," at the extreme end of the Heerengracht, near the beach. No person was permitted to see him except his servant, Thomas Mahony, to bring his meals, who was searched before entering and after leaving the prison, so that no written communications should pass. Several of the inhabitants sent Mr. Edwards his meals daily—so great was the sympathy, and so intense the feeling against Lord Charles Somerset—amongst others the

(From the " S. A. Commercial Advertiser," February 25, 1824.)

WEDNESDAY, FEBRUARY 18, 1824.

Before W. BENTINCK and P. J. TRUTER, Esqrs., as Commissioners of the Court.

HIS MAJESTY'S FISCAL *vs.* LAUNCELOT COOKE, WM. EDWARDS AND J. B. HOFFMAN.

This case, the hearing of which was put off on Monday, the 16th, came on to be further heard this day, and seemed to excite very considerable interest. The avenues leading to the Court were crowded at an early hour. On the assembling of the Court the defendants were not, as before, called in together, but separately.

The proceedings were commenced by the Court calling the first defendant, Mr. L. Cooke, who was asked whether he was willing to answer such *interrogatories* as had been exhibited by the Fiscal.

Mr. Cooke said that previously to answering any questions he had an exception to take to the competency of the Court, which he begged leave to read as follows :—

" I cannot allow this inquiry to be proceeded in without laying before your Worships a true statement of this case, the result of which I doubt not will prove that His Majesty's Fiscal has been premature in bringing this action forward ; that there can exist no grounds for the present action in the present state of this case, and

writer's father The writer frequently accompanied Thomas Mahony when communication was desired, which was done by means of a small dog belonging to Edwards, which wore a broad leather collar. After Mahony and the writer were searched, they were admitted, and the door closed,— the collar was then taken off the dog's neck, and a letter extracted,— another put in by Edwards, the collar replaced, and the servant and the writer departed, after being again searched. Thus was communication carried on from the outer world ; but everything was considered fair, in order to give " fair play " to a man who was considered—whether rightly or wrongly—a victim to oppression and persecution, for no other reason than because he was fearlessly exercising his profession, and could neither be bought nor intimidated.

C 2

that, therefore, this action, *in limine*, ought to be withdrawn from the cognizance of your Worships. I commence by acknowledging what I conceive would be a disgrace to my character to deny, and an insult to the persons whose grievances I thought it necessary to lay before the competent authorities, that I directed to be drawn up, examined, proved and signed the memorial addressed to the Right Honourable the Lords Commissioners of His Majesty's Treasury, treated as libellous by His Majesty's Fiscal, and the subject of the present prosecution. In how far this document may be deemed libellous does not belong to me now to consider, although I trust I shall be able to fully exculpate myself on that head should the principal merits of this case still remain to be discussed hereafter ; but here I beg leave, with the utmost submission, but still with the greatest confidence, to maintain that this document, whether libellous or not, cannot legally, in the present stage of the proceedings, form the subject of a criminal prosecution. Impelled by a sense of duty towards the public, and to several unfortunate subjects, whom I saw the victims of arbitrary power ; become myself the object of violence and insult, because I presumed, in the mildest manner, to advocate the cause of one of those who had faithfully served me for several years, to whom I felt a reciprocal attachment ; and hearing at the same time, from various channels, of similar and worse practices, in the disposal of Negroes, I thought it a duty to them, as well as to Society in general, to represent such cases of which I had proofs in support of my assertion, through the proper official channel, to the constituents of my present accuser, Mr. Blair.

" This memorial is drawn out without the slightest wish to be offensive to His Majesty's Government. It contains an official charge and information solely against Mr. Blair, not affecting his private character, but his public situation as Collector of His Majesty's Customs. The memorial was not published, no publicity whatever was given to it here, and it was only forwarded *to His Excellency the Governor* (with the knowledge of the Collector of Customs) .for the sole purpose of being laid by His Lordship before the proper authorities, as an official impeachment against the Collector of Customs. This memorial was diverted from that channel. The Right Honourable the Lords of the Treasury have not as yet pronounced upon its contents. And I, therefore, beg leave to submit, that it would be prejudging this case, that it would be doing an injury to me and to justice in general—an injury which never could be remedied—were this prosecution allowed to be gone on with, in the face of a charge which has been made officially, from a sense of duty to myself and the public, through the proper channel. and to the proper authorities; a charge which has not as yet been inquired into—for which the time has not yet come to inquire. Upon these grounds, therefore, I beg leave to propose an exception against the legality of this summons, and to pray for an absolution, *ab instantiâ*, with costs."

The Fiscal replied at some length, contending that it was a Libel, and that the Treasury was not the competent authority to which to appeal.

Advocate Cloete, for the first defendant, asked leave of the Court to argue in support of the exception.

The Fiscal objected to it, as being contrary to the 42nd Article of the Crown Trials.

The Court rejected the application of Advocate Cloete, and overruled the exception.

Advocate Cloete, for Mr Cooke, gave notice of appeal against this decision to the full Court.

The first defendant was then *interrogated*, whether he had wilfully, and with a malicious intention, composed, published and signed a certain libellous writing, which was exhibited.

Mr. Cooke admitted that he had signed the memorial, but not with a malicious intention.

He was then *interrogated* as to what he could advance in excuse.

Mr. Cooke requested to be heard by his Advocate, Mr. Cloete, who proposed to conduct his defence by calling some of the witnesses named by the second defendant.

Mr. Edwards, the second defendant, was then called, and informed by the Court that he was at liberty to proceed with his exceptions. He then replied, that on a previous day, in urging his third exception, he asserted "That the Fiscal had stated a detestable falsehood," for which he was committed to prison; that he had been three days in prison, considering the matter, and had not altered his opinion one jot; but for fear of being again incarcerated, he would not further pursue his exception. In support of his fourth exception "as to incompetency of the Court," Mr. Edwards had intended to have urged, that the step which he had taken was the only mode of bringing Mr. Blair to justice; His Excellency the Governor having declared officially, that the Colonial Government had no authority over Mr. Blair in regard to Prize Negroes. He further cited Blackstone, Vol. I., p. 143, showing that in case of uncommon injury, His Majesty's subjects might seek redress by Petition to the King or Parliament. And by Statute I. W. and M. all prosecutions for so petitioning are illegal. He went on to state that Mr. Cooke, himself and Mr. Blair were all natural-born subjects of His Majesty; and cited Blackstone, Vol. I., p. 370, which states "the Prince is always under a constant tie to protect his natural-born subjects, at all times, and in all countries." He cited also "Justinian's Institutes," to prove that any subject, detecting and exposing the malversation of public officers, so far from prosecution, was entitled to certain honours; and that the Fiscal (instead of prosecuting him) had he faithfully discharged his duty, on reading the memorial, should have brought Mr. Blair to trial. He (the Fiscal) boasted in this Court that he had courage to attack any person, however exalted his office, who offended against his duty. Vain boast! Why did he not, when he read the serious charge contained in a memorial from so respectable a gentleman as Mr. Cooke, cause an investigation into the conduct of Mr. Blair, as was done in the case of the Landdrost of Tulbagh? Why did he not prosecute the culprit who intercepted that memorial, if he had so much courage? "I," said Mr. Edwards, "boast no great courage; yet, if you will show me the man who presumed to intercept that complaint to the Lords of the Treasury,—be it Mr. Fiscal, Mr. Blair, or any other Mr.; whatever may be his rank or title,—I will pray the Court to place me in the situation of Fiscal *pro tempore;* we will change places; he will stand where I now do, a prisoner, and I pledge myself, in defiance of every obstacle, to bring the delinquent to justice. Then you shall see, Mr. Fiscal, who has the courage to attack malversation."

The Fiscal replied, in answer to the first exception, that although the summons for personal appearance was granted on the 5th February, yet, as he did not take it from the office until the 9th, he was entitled to calculate the eight days required by the 33rd Art., Crown Trials, from that day. In replying to the second exception, he said that he had submitted to the Court his reasons for not summoning the witnesses for the accused, agreeably to the 8th Art. Many of them were *public officers*, and their attendance would be *inconvenient*. An entire silence he thought the most becoming course with regard to the third exception. As to the fourth, he contended that as Mr. Edwards had in a former case submitted to the jurisdiction of one Commissioner, he could not now object to that of two. He admitted the parties were British subjects, but he did not see that they were consequently entitled to be tried by English law in every part of the globe.

The Court was cleared, and on re-admission, we found that all the exceptions taken by the second defendant were overruled.

Mr. Edwards was then *interrogated*, whether he had wilfully and *mala fide* published, by sending to His Excellency the Governor, the said memorial

Mr. Edwards answered : " I did nothing wilfully nor *mala fide*. I wrote the part of the memorial signed by Mr. Cooke, and sent it to the Lords of the Treasury *bona fide*. I never published it, nor do I know how it was intercepted or came here."

On being asked what he could urge in excuse for it, he answered : " I justify it,—I glory in it. It is the duty of every good subject to inform His Majesty of the malpractices of his servants. I have ever done it, and ever will."

Mr. Hoffman, the third defendant, was then called, and in answer to interrogatories, denied all knowledge of the transaction.

A letter from Mr. W. Bird was here produced by the Fiscal, stating that Mr. Blair was seriously indisposed, and could not attend. The Court, therefore, adjourned the further hearing until Friday.

(Further Proceedings, Friday, Feb. 20th.)

The same degree of interest was excited as on Wednesday. The Court was nearly filled from the commencement; and the further hearing of this case was resumed. The three defendants were all in Court this day.

The Fiscal moved the Court to extend the *whole* charge to the second defendant (Edwards). He said he grounded his application on the defendant's answer to the interrogatories on a former day, and cited the 24th Art. of an English translation of the laws of Demarara, as his authority. He then handed the book over to the defendant, Mr. Edwards. On reading the article, the defendant declared that the Fiscal must be wholly ignorant of the English language, or have wilfully perverted its meaning, the article in question not in the least justifying the conclusion the Fiscal had drawn. He conceived this was a continuation of that system of persecution which had been adopted against him, for doing that which the Fiscal should have done, but which he had not courage to attempt, after Mr. Cooke's complaint had lain dormant in his office for seven or eight weeks. He would take this opportunity of saying, that as it had been alleged that he had treated the Court disrespectfully, he felt it necessary for him to repel so foul an insinuation. He had been bred to the law ; he had been for many years a witness to the impartial administration of justice in his own country, during which time he had learned to honour and revere every honest Magistrate, meet him where he would ; and he would tell the Fiscal, that even in this place he could not shake off his early impressions. In that Court the Fiscal was entitled to no more protection than any other advocate. In his office the Fiscal had offered him a private insult, and the present was the only opportunity of retaliating. " Yes," added Mr. Edwards, "when I was in his office, arguing dispassionately and respectfully against the illegality of his conduct, in intercepting a complaint by one of His Majesty's subjects against one of His Majesty's servants, and that all prosecutions for writing petitions were declared by Stat. 1, W. & M. to be illegal, he burst into an impertinent and intemperate declaration (worse than that for which I was sent to prison—because it was unprovoked, unjust, unlawful and unbecoming) that he would hold no further conversation with me until he met me in Court:—'There,' he said, 'you shall hear me.' Now, had the Fiscal known to whom he addressed that impotent taunt, he would have felt it was dangerous to rouse a lion that will destroy him ; he would have known that I cared as little for his menace as for his persecution or himself; and that in Court—out of Court—at all times—and in any place, I am, at the very, very least, his equal—taking his gown, his influence, his office and his authority into the bargain ;—he would have known there was something in the free, honest, unbending spirit of an English lawyer, not to be insulted with impunity ; he would have known it would take more grates, bars and oppression than he can possess, to tame a soul reared in the lap of liberty ; he would have known that he may manacle my hands, he may shackle my feet, and he may cast my person into a cell ; but I can tell him my soul bids defiance to every Fiscal ; it will soar above him, it will hover over him, it will pounce upon him when and where he least dreams."°

° The writer was in the Court, and perfectly remembers this peroration, and the effect it had upon the listeners. Mr. Edwards was a tall handsome man (an Irishman the writer heard), much resembling the late Mr. Attorney-General Porter in his younger days. There was an irrepressible burst of applause (not, however, reported), and the words have ever since been deeply impressed on the writer's memory. Often and often has he thought of them. On the morning when this scene took place in the Court, " Dreyer's corner " had a number of placards, one of which (copied by the writer) was in doggerel rhyme, as follows :—

> " The bird in yonder cage confined,
>   Thrills thro' me notes of horror:
> A bribe I'll try to bend his mind,
>   And change his tone to-morrow.

> " No, great Fixall, thy fate is known,
>   Thine heart is filled with sorrow ;
> Thou hadst better have left that bird alone,
>   For he will sing thy doom to-morrow."

The Fiscal here interrupted the defendant, and claimed the protection of the Court against expressions so personally directed. Unless he were protected he would not continue to sit there.

The Court was then cleared to deliberate, and on its re-opening Mr. Edwards was informed that the Fiscal's application was refused.

The Fiscal then gave in a list of witnesses, consisting of Mr. C. Blair, Mr. Wilberforce Bird, Mr. Ponterdent, Mr. Tyrholm, Mr. Lind and Mr. Bendall. The two latter were to prove the memorial was copied by Mr. Hoffman; Mr. Tyrholm to prove that Jean Elle (the Prize Negro referred to in the memorial) had been his servant on his first landing, and, after some years, was restored to the Collector of Customs for ill-conduct; the three first were to prove the *falsehood* of the memorial.

Mr. Edwards here objected to evidence being called to prove anything *not charged in the indictment ;* it not being therein once alleged that any part of the memorial was untrue. On the contrary, the indictment says "that the memorial was written seemingly with the intention to bring to the cognizance of the Lords of the Treasury Mr. Cooke's complaint against the Collector of Customs, requesting them to cause an investigation thereof, and afford him redress ; and that he did also, with the intention to expose the officers of Customs to the hatred and contempt of their superiors, and to bring them in danger of being ignominiously discharged from their situations, make remarks and allege facts by which they are represented in a contemptible and criminal aspect." He then argued that inasmuch as the assertions in the memorial were admitted to be "facts,"—and as facts are truths, he could hardly conceive how any man, pretending to be a lawyer, would attempt to call witnesses to prove that his own assertions were *false.* He had no objection that Mr. Blair, Mr. Bird and Mr. Ponterdent should be called to prove the truth of the memorial, as out of their own mouths he would convict them. He admitted that Jean Elle had served Mr. Tyrholm faithfully while a prisoner of war, but on the war terminating he became a free man, and was no longer willing to serve as a slave. He thought it a novel thing to bring a writing master to prove Mr. Hoffman's handwriting, and upon that proof prosecute him ;—the paper-maker, or the goose whence the pen with which it was written was plucked, might as well be prosecuted.

The Court called on Mr. Edwards to say what was the purport of the proofs he wished to produce. He answered, he was prepared to prove the truth of *everything* contained in the memorial, and much more.

The defendant then asked the Fiscal whether he had not communicated a list of his (defendant's) witnesses to Mr. Blair. The Fiscal refused to answer.

Mr. Edwards stated that this refusal, in his opinion, proved the fact ; and as the Fiscal would not answer he could tell the Court that this list had been exhibited to Mr. Blair, who had taken advantage of it by tampering with some of his (the defendant's) witnesses. He would put this question to Mr. Blair on his oath ; if he denied it, by the evidence of two witnesses he was prepared to prove it to the Court.

The Court intimated to the defendant that if he could prove what he asserted, he might proceed against the Fiscal and Mr. Blair.

The defendant replied he was aware when and how to seek for justice. But he knew better than to assail a snake in its own hiding place. It was nothing encouraging to him to be told by the same breath which sent him to prison for exposing the Fiscal's falsehood that he might prosecute him for it. He then declared that he had already petitioned the House of Commons against the unjust and unlawful proceedings the Fiscal had adopted. " *Here,*" said he, " the Fiscal sits dressed in all possible power—*there* he will appear a culprit ; and I not only received as a man of well-known character, but as an undaunted patriot. My character will place me as far above him there as he is here above the lowest menial of this Court."

The Court was cleared for deliberation, and on re-admission it was adjudged *that no witnesses should be examined as to the truth or untruth of the memorial.* Mr. Advocate Cloete, for Mr. Cooke, appealed against this decision, as did Mr. Edwards.

Mr. Edwards then stated that at the best of times he was unable to bear the expenses of this prosecution, he was the less able to do so in prison, having little but the honest earnings of his business to support him. He, therefore, prayed the Court to grant him an advocate to plead *pro Deo*, and also to have copies of papers, &c., free from Court fees.

The Court required a certificate of his inability to defray the expense, which being made, we understand Mr. Advocate Brand was nominated.

[Messrs. Lind and Bendall being called, the case against Mr. Hoffman broke down, and the Court, after a short deliberation, pronounced him *acquitted*.]

(*From the* "*S. A. Commercial Advertiser*," *March* 3, 1824.)

MONDAY, FEBRUARY 26, 1824.

HIS MAJESTY'S FISCAL *vs.* LAUNCELOT COOKE AND WM. EDWARDS.

On appeal to the Full Court° (with the exception of Sir JOHN TRUTER, Chief Justice, who was out of town).

Long prior to the opening of the Court, every avenue was crowded, and an expression of the deepest interest pervaded every countenance. On the Court being opened, the rush was tremendous; in a few moments every place affording the least chance of hearing was occupied.

* The Full Court was composed of eight members under the Dutch Constitution, as it existed until the year 1828, with a Chief Justice as its head. There was also a final Court of Appeal, over which the Governor presided. There were some amusing anecdotes told of some of the members of the Court, one of which was as follows:—A member, it was said, was very fond of Fish, *boiled*; his lady, on the contrary, liked it *fried*. On the occasion of a trial in a rather serious case, the member referred to, when the Court was cleared for deliberation, had fallen into a doze, and awaking up suddenly as from a dream, called out aloud "Let the half be *boiled* and the half *fried*." Whether this referred to the *fish*, or the *prisoner*, was not said.

The proceedings were commenced by Mr. Advocate Brand, who rose to argue in favour of the exceptions taken by the defendant Mr. Edwards on a former day, and which having been overruled by the Court below, were appealed from to the Full Court.

[The arguments of Counsel, and the replies of the Fiscal, will appear in our next.] *

Mr. Advocate Cloete, who appeared for Mr. Cooke, in the course of his argument read the memorial which gave rise to the prosecution.

The *South African Commercial Advertiser* of the 10th March, 1824, contains the arguments of Advocates Brand and Cloete, occupying a very large space, and too long to be here inserted.

The Court, after some deliberation, confirmed the sentence of the Commissioners.

The defendant (Mr. Edwards) then entered a further appeal against this decision ; so that it must now be finally heard before His Excellency the Governor, in the Court of Appeals.

The Court then proceeded to hear the appeal entered by the defendant Cooke, from the decrees of the Court on the 11th and 20th instant, in rejecting his exception of incompetency ; and in refusing to admit any witnesses either for or against the defendants.

The argument of Advocate Cloete and reply of the Fiscal having been heard, the Court, after deliberating for a short time, confirmed the sentences appealed from, and condemned the first defendant, Mr. Cooke, in all prior expenses ; and fixed the costs in this appeal at Fifteen Rix-dollars (£1 2s. 6d.).

The Fiscal and the defendants severally appealed against the determination of the Court in refusing to go into the examination of any witnesses whatever.

* The argument of Mr. Advocate Brand (the late Speaker of the House of Assembly, Sir Christopher) is given in full in the following number of the *S. A. Commerical Advertiser*, and is a masterpiece of forensic eloquence. It, as well as the subsequent able argument of Advocate Cloete, are omitted here, in consequence of their great length.

Immediately under the report, as concluded in the above paragraph, appears the following, apparently Editorial :—

REMARKABLE OCCURRENCE.—Several LIES were lost on the Heerengracht last week.

———

The *S. A. Commercial Advertiser* of the 31st March, 1824, contains the report of the Conclusion of the Trial, as follows :—

FRIDAY, MARCH 26, 1824.

Before W. BENTINCK and P. J. TRUTER, Esqrs., as Commissioners of the Court.

HIS MAJESTY'S FISCAL *vs.* L. COOKE AND W. EDWARDS.

The Full Court having, on the 26th February, refused to hear witnesses either in support of or against the allegations contained in the memorial which was the subject of the suit :—the Fiscal and the defendants severally appealed to the Court of Appeals, which, after some lapse of time, rejected the case, and referred it back to the Court below to try the merits of the alleged Libel.

The decision of the Court of Appeals was read, and the parties were informed that the case was to proceed.

The Fiscal submitted to the Court that he wished to call two witnesses (Mr. J. H. Whitton and Mr. G. Thompson) whose names did not appear in the list already exhibited, he having only learnt of the publication of the memorial to them on the 26th February.

By their evidence he intended to prove that the memorial had been published previously to its transmission to the Governor by Mr. Edwards. The defendants having already admitted sending the duplicate of the memorial to His Excellency was sufficient proof for him of its publication ; but the evidence of the two witnesses he had named, although he did not deem it ot much consequence to establish the fact, would serve more fully to substantiate it.

Mr. Edwards exclaimed :—" Another misrepresentation ! I am surprised," said he, " to see the Fiscal recur to his former system of misstating facts. I deny having ever admitted that I sent the memorial to Lord Charles Somerset. When I was interrogated by the Court I acknowledged no more than having sent it to the Lords of the Treasury ; therefore this pretended admission by the Fiscal is false ; and I beg the Secretary may enter on the record that this is my opinion. Let the Fiscal, however, bring forward these witnesses—I do not object to their examination."

Advocate Cloete, for Mr. Cooke, called the attention of the Court to the train of informal and illegal proceedings which the Fiscal had been guilty of during the whole course of this trial, and said that the present application was another striking instance of that disregard to rules and orders which substantially secure the ends of justice. The Fiscal is aware that by the 38th and 41st Articles of the Crown Trials, the names of the whole of the witnesses required during the prosecution must be delivered in at the first opening of the trial, and that none others may afterwards be allowed, except for the most urgent reasons. The Fiscal is aware that both parties appealed from the decree of the Court rejecting the production of *any* witnesses, even of those whom the Fiscal had thought necessary, in the first instance, in support of the action. That decree stands confirmed by the Full Court, and by that of the Court of Appeals ; and, in the face of the standing rules of the Courts of Law, and of the express decree in this particular case, the present application is made. The Fiscal moreover admits that he only heard of these witnesses on the 26th of February ; they could not therefore be of so much consequence as to tend to support an action which had been brought on the 16th of that month, although it appears rather late now to think of the proceedings when final judgment is already expected by the parties. But the acknowledgment in the prayer of the Fiscal betrays the impossibility of his request being attended to, for he admits that these witnesses are not strictly wanted by him, while the 21st Article of the Crown Trials forbids any being heard in an after stage of the proceedings, except on the most weighty con-

siderations ; and should those now named by the Fiscal still be
necessary to prove any publicity, the defendant would be under
the necessity of producing others to prove the contrary. Upon
these grounds he (Mr. Cloete) submitted that the prayer of the
Fiscal should be dismissed.

The Court was then cleared for deliberation, in which it was for
a considerable time engaged. On our re-admission, we found the
sentence of the Court to be—that the application of the Fiscal
was rejected, on the ground that during the course of this prosecution no new or unforeseen facts had been brought forward which
could in any way warrant the introduction of new witnesses ; and
decreed *all further investigation of this case to be at an end.* Released
the defendants from further personal appearance, and *wholly acquitted*
them of the charges contained in the indictment.

Mr. Edwards said : " In one stage of this investigation, when I
was objecting to the conduct of the Fiscal, your Worships told me
that if he had done wrong in prosecuting me, or in intercepting
the memorial, I was as much at liberty to prosecute him as he to
prosecute me. You have now declared that this action is ground-
less. I would, therefore, ask—Where is my remedy for all the
persecution that has been heaped upon me ? For having been sent
to prison ? For having been held up as a criminal by the Fiscal ;
And for having been insulted by a threat in the indictment of
suffering corporal punishment ? "—when he was interrupted by the
Court, who said they had now discharged their duties, and if Mr.
Edwards felt aggrieved he could apply to any authority he thought
fit for redress."

It will be seen that this "sentence of the Court," as it is
called in the report, was given on Friday, the 26th March,
1824, and the report appeared in the thirteenth number of the
Commercial Advertiser, printed on the following Wednesday,
the 31st March. In the next number, No. 14, printed on the
7th April, 1824, appeared a " leading article " which, although
not *directly* referring to the recent trial, was so heavy a blow at
the prevailing despotism, that it sealed the fate, as will be seen

in the sequel, of the *Commercial Advertiser.* The article, which was written by Mr. Pringle, is here transcribed :—

" Whoever in this empire is tied by no other rules than *his own will* and lust, must either be a Saint or else a very Devil incarnate ; or if he be neither of these, both his life and his reign are like to be very short. For whoever takes upon him so execrable an employment as to rule men against the laws of nature and reason, must turn all topsy turvy, and never stick at anything ; for, if he once halt, he will fall never to rise again ; and so I bid you heartily farewell."—*Machiavel's Vindication of Himself and His Writings, &c.*— Harleian Miscellany, Vol. I., page 66.

" With this passage Machiavel concludes his very able defence against the charge of having instructed tyrants to rule with despotic sway. He admits that, if writing a true history of the arts by which political eminence has generally been attained amongst an enslaved people can be considered a proof of his guilt, he has deserved punishment ; but pleads his having, at the same time, taught the people how to prevent the growth of arbitrary power, as an alleviation of his crime, which, we think, amongst a free and intelligent people, should entitle him to a pardon.

" *Divide and Govern* is the maxim of the Machiavelian School, by which despotism has been fostered in Independent States. But, in Provinces, as the established power is always dependent on external support, their rulers have seldom had occasion to sow among the people the seeds of division. It is by the observance of the opposite rule—the UNITE *and Govern* yourselves—that liberty has been preserved or re-established in every country where it now exists ; and it is a remedy of such efficacy, that no Government has yet been found capable of resisting, for any protracted period, the united voice of Public Opinion. But how are discordant opinions to be assimilated ? How are weak prejudices to be overcome ? And how are a body of people, who have exactly the same interests, to be brought to feel in the same way ? It can only be done by an open discussion of the differences that exist. We repeat, *it is only to be effected by means of a Free Press.*

" That some shades of difference in the feelings of the inha-

D

bitants of this Colony are to be discovered we have no reason to doubt. That there is a great difference of opinion as to the best means of attaining every desirable end, every one knows to be the case; and so it ought to be. But we maintain that, on every important point connected with the public interest, there is only one wish entertained by the Honest and Independent, from one end of the Colony to the other. For instance :—Every one wishes to see an individual of liberal principles, of exalted family and independent fortune, and if possible, without much family influence at home—and a civilian—placed at the head of the Government. Every one wishes that the power of the Governor to infringe on Private Liberty, as well as the influence of the Government, may be reduced as far as is consistent with the public safety. Every one desires to know, at least, the laws by which we are to be governed in future, and to see them administered by an *independent* as well as an enlightened and impartial Bench of Judges. Every one wishes to see the Revenue derived from the least objectionable sources, and the expenditure reduced to what is necessary, on an economical scale, for the support of a respectable establishment ; and especially of a strict Police. For we have no partiality, at the Cape, for the Roudies, Dirkers and Gougers of the Backwoods of America. But, above all, in order to secure these advantages when we have got them, and to guard against abuse of every description, every honest man desires that public measures may be open to discussion, and that it may be lawful for him to speak or write what he pleases, so long as he does no injury to his neighbour ; or in other words, that the Liberty (not the Licentiousness) of the Press may be protected by Law.

" By factious motives we never are, nor ever can be, actuated in this Colony, under the present system of Government. A FACTION is a combination of a number of persons to promote exclusively their ambitious or interested views, opposed to PARTY, where public principle is the bond of union. But who ever heard of a faction consisting of the majority of the inhabitants of a country ? What could any one gain here by entering into such a conspiracy against the interest of his fellow subjects ? He could not expect, in this Colony, to get into power by pushing others out of their places, and, perhaps, he could not take a more certain means of depriving himself of the countenance of even a good Government, than by adventuring to expose the errors of a bad one. Such are the usual and pernicious effects of undefined power on the human understanding and feelings.

"If, however, any faction does exist at this moment in this Colony, we may, without fear of contradiction, assure the public that it does not consist of the enemies of the established system.

"When we consider the notoriety of a great part of what we have now stated, we cannot help indulging a smile at the weakness of those who attempt to impose upon strangers, by telling them dismal stories of extensive combinations against the quiet and *decent order of things* established here; and who tell every one, in a whining tone, that there is an end to harmony at the Cape which we all recollect; when it might have been said—without any very extravagant hyperbole—not a bird durst perch upon a bush and sing, without the leave of the Colonial Government."

In the same number of the *Commercial Advertiser* appeared extracts from a work, printed the previous year in England, entitled "State of the Cape of Good Hope in 1822. By a Civil Servant." Especially did these extracts dwell on the "*Liberty of the Press*," as a corrective of Despotism, and the vices and absurdities of mankind,—and expressing surprise that, in Cape Town, individuals have not established a press as a private concern. In the next numbers, 10 and 17, April 21 and 28, 1824, similar extracts appeared from De Lolme's excellent work on the Constitution of England, on the advantages of a "Free Press," and from an old work on the Cape by J. S. Stavorinus, Rear-Admiral in the service of the States-General.

The utter collapse of the trial of Messrs Cooke, Edwards and Hoffman,—the scathing addresses of Advocates Brand and Cloete in defending two of the defendants,—the leading article of the *South African Commercial Advertiser* of the 7th April,

1824,—the unflinching front shown by the able (though indiscreet) Mr. Edwards,—and the dignified and independent tone of Messrs. John Fairbairn and Thomas Pringle—the Editors of the *Advertiser*—were as gall and wormwood to the despot who had during eleven years ruled the Cape Colony with a rod of iron. The doom of the paper was sealed,—only Phœnix-like to rise from its ashes with greater splendour. But this last act of tyranny also proved the downfall of the Governor.

No. 18 of the *South African Commercial Advertiser* appeared on the 5th May, 1824, with the following

"POSTSCRIPT."

"WEDNESDAY MORNING, ONE O'CLOCK.

"His Majesty's Fiscal having assumed the CENSORSHIP of the *South African Commercial Advertiser* by an Official Order, sent to the printing office by a messenger late in the evening before publication, demanding *proof sheets* of the paper for next day [this day] and prohibiting its being struck off 'till we had received his further instructions thereon,' we find it our duty, as BRITISH SUBJECTS, under these circumstances, to discontinue the publication of the said paper, *for the present*, in this Colony, until we have applied for redress and direction to His Excellency the Governor and the British Government.

"Our numerous subscribers will, we trust, require no further explanation at present of this distressing interruption. They, and the rest of the world, shall be speedily put in possession of a full statement of all the FACTS:—one of which is a demand from the Fiscal of Two Securities, on or before Friday next, to become bound, under a penalty of TEN THOUSAND RIXDOLLARS [£750] that nothing *offensive* shall appear in any future number—such as extracts from the experienced work of the Civil Servant, a work PUBLISHED in this Colony, this year, by W. W. Bird, Esq., *Comptroller of Customs, and Assessor of the Court of Appeals.*

"We will only mention further, at present, that not a word of this our last number has been written, or *altered*, in consequence of the abovementioned transactions, excepting this notice."

The following extract from Mr. Pringle's account of this tyrannical proceeding is taken from his book :—" The crisis having thus arrived, · Mr. Fairbairn and I explained to· Mr. Greig the course we had determined to pursue, namely, never to compromise our birthright as British subjects by editing any publication under a censorship. But we advised him to weigh maturely all the consequences, and either act upon our principles, or continue the newspaper without us, as he might judge best. Mr. Greig, however, declared himself resolved to follow the same course, and announced next morning, in our last paper, that in consequence of the Fiscal's assumption of the censorship, the publication would be discontinued until the decision of His Majesty's Government on the subject should be ascertained."

The leading article of this the eighteenth and last number of the *Commercial Advertiser*, being a review of the work of Barrow on the Cape of Good Hope, concludes with the following passages—sentiments which, though written *Sixty Years Ago*, are equally applicable to the present time—(November, 1884), and worthy to be recorded : —

"To the Dutch colonists, now our countrymen and fellow-subjects, we particularly address the following remarks. However much they may occasionally be galled or exasperated by the unfair or unfeeling sarcasms of English travellers or journalists, they may rest assured that the regards of the Government and generous people of England are ever directed towards them with indulgent liberality and affection. Let authors be judged of by their words ; but nations and governments only by their actions England, of all nations that ever existed, pursues the most liberal system of policy towards the countries she has won or nurtured. Her Ministers, no doubt, are fallible, like other men ; and they have sometimes erred in regard to the administration of the Colonies, and may possibly err again—*but it must be from ignorance of the truth*, if the British Government ever does, or permits deliberate injustice to be done towards any part or appendage of the Empire. This Colony, *if abandoned by England, would fall an easy prey to the first rapacious tyrant that chose to seize it.* Under her free and fostering guardianship alone may we rationally hope to attain permanent prosperity, liberty and happiness.

"Let, therefore, no temporary vexations, nor any possible accumulation of private annoyances, ever for a moment disturb the perfect reliance,—or weaken the firm loyalty of our fellow-subjects (whether Dutch or English) towards the wise, just and beneficent Government of England. Is she not doing for us all we have ever asked of her—and more ? Has she not sent out able and honourable men to inquire into our local grievances, disadvantages and restrictions; and who are at this moment traversing the remotest districts of our country, to hear and see and report upon whatever requires to be amended ? Whoever now sits sulkily down and broods fretfully over his wrongs or disadvantages, instead of availing himself of the regular and legitimate channel which has been consistently opened for their redress, deserves to bear them, for ever, unpitied—and can never hereafter ascribe the fault to the neglect of the British Government.

"Above all, let all good and patriotic citizens beware of any intemperance, in word or deed, towards any individual to whom the legal authority of Government has been delegated. We are FREEMEN ; and, if any of our Rulers do oppression or wrong, they can be called to answer for it at the bar of their country, as well as the meanest of their fellow-subjects : but their office and persons ought to be duly respected so long as they continue to occupy the stations to which our gracious Sovereign has been pleased to promote them. If there be any persons in the Colony (we trust there are none) who would teach men *disrespect* to even the shadow of LEGAL AUTHORITY, let good citizens beware of them. Fools and desperadoes may talk or act intemperately : wise and patriotic men ought to be distinguished by candour, calmness and self-possession."

What a noble closing to the *S. A. Commercial Advertiser !*

Two days before the publication of the 18th number of the
S. A. Commercial Advertiser, viz , on the 3rd May, 1824, the
Fiscal sent for Mr. Greig. " This officer (the Fiscal)," writes
Mr. Greig, "speaks the English language with something of a
foreign accent, and perhaps with something of a foreign idiom ;
English ears, therefore, are not always sudden'y possessed of his
meaning. And the person who owns these ears,* and entertains
a prudent respect for them, should, when suddenly called before
so important a magistrate,—who, to use the phrase of the
' Civil Servant,' is invested with some very odious privileges—
an Englishman, we say, should, in such cases, implore the Fiscal
to express his will in writing, to prevent after *mistakes* or
misstatements " Accordingly, Mr. Greig, on his return from
his interview, addressed the subjoined note to His Majesty's
Fiscal :—

" Commercial Printing Office, May 3, 1824.

" D. DENYSSEN, Esq.

" SIR,—On my return home this afternoon, after the conversation
I held with you at your house, in Strand-street, I found it impossible
to charge my memory with the main circumstances which trans-
pired. I have, therefore, to request you will favour me with a
wr tten statement of any instructions or documents which you have
had communicated to you with reference to the subject you urged·
It must be unnecessary for me to point out the impracticability
of acting upon verbal communications from any public functionary
whatever. Your early answer to this is requested."

" I have, &c.,

" (Signed)   GEO. GREIG."

To which His Majesty's Fiscal sent the following reply :—

" Cape Town, 3rd May, 1824.

" To Mr. GEO. GREIG.

" SIR,—In reply to your letter just received, I cannot but refer
you to the communication I have been instructed to make to you

---

° The above was written at the time by Mr. Greig in " Facts connected
with the stopping of the S. A. Commercial Advertiser."

on the subject of your having deviated from the terms of your prospectus of the *South African Commercial Advertiser.* If any further explanation is required application may be made for the same to His Excellency, through the usual medium of the Colonial Secretary.

" I have the honour, &c.,

"(Signed)   D. DENYSSEN, Fiscal."

In this stage of the business, Tuesday, the 4th May, arrived, and about eight o'clock in the evening, while all was bustle and preparation in the *Commercial Printing Office*, a messenger from the Fiscal entered, and delivered to Mr. Greig the following note :—

"No. 11, Strand-street, May 4, 1824.

"To Mr. GEORGE GREIG, Commercial Printing Office.

" Sir,—I hope that you will have no objection to send me a Proof Sheet of your 18th Number of the *South African Commercial Advertiser,* previous to its being struck off. Your immediate reply will much oblige me.

" I have the honour, &c.,

"(Signed)   D. DENYSSEN, Fiscal."

To this Mr. Greig sent the following reply :—

"Sir,—I have the honour to acknowledge your note of to-night, as follows :—'I hope that you will have no objection to send me a Proof Sheet of your 18th Number of the *South African Commercial Advertiser,* previous to its being struck off. Your immediate reply will much oblige me.'

"To this note, I have the honour to state in answer, that I am ready to comply, with promptitude, to every 'Official Order.'

" (Signed)   GEORGE GREIG."

The messenger quickly returned, and served and duly delivered a copy of the following Official Order, the same being required:—

"MESSENGER.—You are to require Mr. G. Greig forthwith to deliver to you a Proof Sheet of his 18th Number of the Weekly

Paper, entitled *The South African Commercial Advertiser*, and not to allow the same to be struck off until he shall have received my further directions thereon. Serve and duly deliver a Copy of this Official Order, if required ; and relate the answer of Mr. Greig in writing.

"(Signed)   D. DENYSSEN, Fiscal.

W. MILLS, Es. Messenger.

" Cape Town, 4th May, 1824."

All the proof sheets then ready were immediately sent in obedience to the Official Order of the Fiscal. In about an hour the Fiscal sent an IMPRIMATUR, as follows :—

"Cape Town, 4th May, 1824.

"Mr. G. GREIG,—Sir,—I have no objection to your going on in printing the pages of your 18th Number now in my possession, viz. : the first page, and the pages 146, 147, 148 and 149, which, however, I hope, will not be construed as an approval of that part thereof which bears upon the administration of this Colony, such as the 1st column of page 146,* nor as an approval of Mr. Fairplay's letter.

" I am, &c.,

" (Signed)   D. DENYSSEN, Fiscal."

The remaining proof sheets being now ready, were sent to the Fiscal with the following note :—

" May 4, 1824.

"Sir,—Merely to save time, I send these proofs of No. 18 of my Paper, by my own servant, in consequence of your previous Official Order ; your messenger not having waited, as desired by me, till they were ready. I accompany them with this note in order to have an opportunity of stating that my sending you proofs previous to publication is not a voluntary act on my part, but an act of obedience to authority.

" I have the honour, &c.,

" (Signed)   GEORGE GREIG."

*The excellent leading article, from which extracts will be found.

On the following morning came the second IMPRIMATUR, as follows :—

"The Fiscal having perused the remaining pages of the eighteenth number of the *South African Commercial Advertiser*, although he does not think himself justified to approve the whole of its contents, will allow its being printed."—Strand-street, 5th May, 1824.

"MR. GEORGE GREIG."

The eighteenth number was printed on the morning of the 5th May, 1824, precisely as it was intended, before the interference of the Fiscal, not a single alteration or omission having taken place, with the exception of the "Postscript," signifying its being suspended for the present.

The Fiscal having denied that he had demanded security for Ten Thousand Rixdollars of Mr. Greig, the latter gave his version of the conversation which took place at the Fiscal's house on the 3rd May : —

"On Monday evening, the Fiscal sent a messenger to me, requesting I would call at his house in Strand-street. I did so. He then opened a conversation upon the subject of my paper—the *South African Commercial Advertiser*, and said he was *instructed* to inform me that I had departed from the Prospectus ;—that it had become obnoxious to the Government, and referred more particularly to the last three or four numbers. I asked him to point out such parts as were immediately objectionable. He then mentioned some *leading remarks*, which he said bore upon the Administration of the Colony. He further pointed out, as *obnoxious*, all quotations which had been made from 'De Lolme,' Blackstone, the 'Civil Servant's' works, 'Lacon,' and generally all extracts relative to the '*Liberty of the Press*,' observing—'nobody can doubt the *obvious tendency* of these ; and as we are not men in this Colony, but merely infants,' it was, in his opinion, dangerous to insert such matter. He added, also, that it was expected I should, in future, publish *no parts* of Trials, but wait until the whole were finished ; and, *even then*, all *scurrilous* parts (such as the memorial of Mr. L. Cooke to the Treasury) were to be *omitted*. That I was further to be bound down with Two Sureties, in the Penalty of Ten Thousand Rixdollars, that *nothing* of the offensive nature pointed out should appear in any future number ; and lastly, that I was to take particular care that the next number (18) contained no matter of the description alluded to, *nor any notice of Mr. Edwards' trial*. To all this I replied that I would give no promise as to what would appear in the next or any future number. That I required time to consider what was fitting to be done with regard to the security demanded. The Fiscal then named Friday morning. I requested a copy of the instructions upon which he professed to act. He then dictated as from a paper which lay before him, but refused a perfect copy. The Fiscal said he had my memorial before him, which he read to me, and on my directing his attention to the *answer* which had been given to me, he professed himself totally ignorant of the existence of any answer. On my arrival home I thought it improper to trust to, or act upon, *any verbal* communication from a Public Servant, and therefore addressed a note to the Fiscal, requesting a copy of any document or instructions he had upon the subject. This the Fiscal refused, but referred me to the Governor, through the usual medium of the Colonial Secretary. That the substance of this is true, I am ready to make affidavit.

"(Signed)   GEORGE GREIG."

The *S. A. Commercial Advertiser* having ceased to exist with the eighteenth number, on Wednesday, the 5th May, 1824, on account of the proprietor refusing to submit to the attempted CENSORSHIP of the Fiscal—or rather of Lord Charles Somerset—Mr Greig forwarded to the *Government Gazette* the following two *advertisements*, for publication, on the usual terms of payment, but were *refused insertion* :—

"TRIAL OF MR. EDWARDS.

"The Trial of Mr. Edwards, now pending before the Commissioners of the Worshipful Court of Justice, together

with all Official Proceedings connected with that subject, will be
fully reported for publication, after the close of the proceedings.
To be printed and published in London. Orders for this interesting publication may now be sent to Mr. Geo. Greig, 30, Longmarket-street, Cape Town, in order to prevent after disappointment
and to regulate him in regard to the number required for the supply
of the Cape Market.

    " Commercial Printing Office,
        " No. 30, Longmarket-street, Cape Town."

The following is Mr. Greig's version of the trial of Wm.
Edwards, in a memorial addressed to Earl Bathurst, H.M.
Secretary of State for Colonial Affairs:—

" The immediate reason which led to the paper's suppression may
be traced without hazarding much conjecture. The Governor
might entertain apprehensions that the *trial* of Mr. Edwards would
be published. The gross exposures which were made in the course
of that trial seriously involved his (the Governor's) character and that
of others, and these circumstances might render the Governor particularly anxious that the proceedings should be suppressed ; but if
it be intended to be held or asserted that this furnished a sufficient
ground for annihilating my trade, ruining my prospects, and stamp-
ing my character with the charge of 'seditious,' I rest satisfied that
that position will not meet with your Lordship's sanction. As the
case of Mr. Edwards is, I understand, to be brought before the
House of Commons, all that I will state to your Lordship respecting
his trial is, that although Mr. Edwards upon oath denied all knowledge of the letter charged as libellous, the Court of Justice, without calling or permitting him to call a single witness, found him
guilty, and sentenced him to seven years' transportation, a course of
proceeding to prevent the promulgation of which the anxiety of the
Governor is not to be wondered at. Two hours after the adjourn-
ment of the Court, at eight o'clock on the evening previous to publication, came the letter of the Fiscal requiring proof sheets of my

next paper ; and the subsequent acts of which I complain continued till the *Sunday* following, the day on which my presses were sealed up, myself charged with sedition, and ordered to be banished from the Colony."

"NOTICE TO THE PUBLIC.

"On Wednesday next a Paper, containing advertisements only, will be published at the above Office and forwarded for the accommodation of our Commercial Friends, to the Subscribers to the *South African Commercial Advertiser*, at present suspended on account of the Fiscal's attempt to assume the Censorship of it.

"Here we stand at present. When the matter is closed, we will not forget our pledge of letting the world know all the *facts* connected with our distressing interruption.

"Commercial Printing Office, 30, Longmarket-st., Cape Town."

These two advertisements having been refused insertion in the *Government Gazette* by the " Censor " of that interesting publication, the second of them was printed at the *Commercial Printing Office* as a hand-bill, and posted in the usual way by order of Mr. Greig, together with another, of which the following is a copy :—

"AUDI ALTERAM PARTEM."

"On Monday morning, at eight o'clock, will be published—

"FACTS,

"Connected with the Stopping of the Press, and the Censorship of the Fiscal.

"*South African Commercial Advertiser* Office,
30, Longmarket-street, Cape Town."

In about an hour after these were posted, a person came to Mr. Greig's premises, and commenced tearing down these placards. He was, however, prevented, and retired. Mr.

Greig immediately waited on the Fiscal, to inquire whether he had issued orders for this attack on his premises and property. The Deputy-Fiscal, who was on duty, replied in the affirmative, but refused to give any written document ; upon which Mr. Greig returned to his office, and gave orders to his people to discontinue the publication of the hand-bills. He continued, however, to arrange the " Statement of Facts," connected with the stopping of his paper, and the Censorship of the Fiscal, which he was thus prohibited from advertising. It was all got into type, and prepared to be thrown off and published on the Monday morning following. But on the intervening *Sabbath*, about 3 o'clock p.m., His Majesty's Fiscal, with the Sheriffs, and a Commission from the Worshipful Court of Justice, entered Mr. Greig's premises, and read the following warrant :—

"By His Excellency the Right Honourable General Lord CHARLES HENRY SOMERSET, one of His Majesty's Most Honourable Privy Council, Colonel of His Majesty's 1st West India Regiment, Governor and Commander-in-Chief of His Majesty's Castle, Town and Settlement of the Cape of Good Hope, in South Africa, and the Territories and Dependencies thereof, and Ordinary and Vice-Admiral of the same, Commander of the Forces, &c., &c., &c.

"Whereas GEORGE GREIG, by special permission of His Majesty's Government, Printer of the *South African Commercial Advertiser*, in this Colony, has not only openly transgressed the conditions under which such permission has been granted to him, but has moreover wantonly and *seditiously* persisted in doing so, after having been warned by His Majesty's Fiscal, and in the name of the Colonial Government been required to give security for the due observance of the said conditions ;—Wherefore, and in order to prevent the evil consequences which, from any further forbearance, might accrue to the peace and tranquility of the Colony, you are hereby authorized and directed, with the assistance of a Commission from the

Worshipful the Court of Justice, t o repair to the Printing Office of the said George Greig, No. 30, Longmarket-street, and there, in the name of His Majesty's Government, to prohibit the said George Greig continuing to act as publisher of the *South African Commercial Advertiser*; and further, in the presence of the Commission to seal up all and every *press*, or *presses*, of him the said George Greig, in order to remain so sealed up until His Majesty's pleasure shall be known.

"And whereas the personal conduct of the said George Greig has proved subversive of that due submission to the lawful commands of the Constituted Authorities in this Colony, without which peace and tranquillity cannot remain undisturbed, you are further authorized and directed to notify to him, the said George Greig, that he is to leave the Colony within one month from the date hereof, and that in default of so doing he shall be arrested and sent out of it by the first suitable opportunity.

"Given under my hand and Seal, at the Cape of Good-Hope, this Eighth Day of May, One Thousand Eight Hundred and Twenty-four.

"L.S. (Signed) CHARLES HENRY SOMERSET.

"By His Excellency's Command,

"(Signed) P. G. BRINK, Assistant Sec. to Government.

"To D. DENYSSEN, Esq., H.M. Fiscal.

"A true Copy.—D. DENYSSEN, Fiscal.

"Endorsed (in Dutch) by the Chief Justice, Sir JOHN TRUTER, authorizing the Commission to see the Warrant executed."

It will be seen that the preamble to this warrant is a mass of misstatements. Mr. Greig never had the "permission of His Majesty's Government"; on the contrary, he was *refused* permission; he never entered into any "conditions," his prospectus was a voluntary act; he never committed, nor was ever charged with, any act of "sedition"; he never

" persisted " in disobeying any official order of the Fiscal, but on the contrary studiously " obeyed "; and the Fiscal himself *denied*, by letter in the *Government Gazette*, that he had called upon Mr. Greig to enter into security for ten thousand rixdollars. So that the whole of the preamble was wilfully untrue, and these misstatements were signed by the Governor of the Colony! And all this took place during the first quarter of the nineteenth century! How much do editors and the public of the present day owe to the brave men who so manfully and so uncompromisingly battled for, and eventually gained, the incalculable victory of the " Free Press " of South Africa! It was even said that the Governor was seen in the vicinity of Mr. Greig's premises when the press was being sealed up.*

The writer was present, and an eye-witness of what followed after the warrant was read. Mr. Greig showed the Fiscal into the press-room and pointed out the best way of preventing the press being used (by fastening the " bar-handle " to the " cheek," with red tape and a seal). " Thank you," said the Fiscal, " *we are not in the habit of sealing-up presses.*" One member of the Commission placed his hand on the inking frame, and

---

° The following are Mr. Greig's remarks on the " *Warrant* " in his Memorial to Earl Bathurst:—" I now, my Lord, proceed to the examination of the Warrant itself; and as it is the principal measure of which I complain, the act hurled ruin and defamation upon me, I beg to append a copy of it. The Warrant commences with a wholly untrue assertion. It says: ' Whereas George Greig, by special permission of His Majesty's Government, printer of the *South African Commercial Advertiser*,' &c. So far, my Lord, from any ' special permission ' having been granted, I have already stated that *no application* was ever made to the Colonial Government on the subject, nor could they have been aware of my intention until the paper was publicly announced; thus the very reason which the Governor assigns, in the preamble to this Warrant, for resorting to such a step, is wholly unfounded; the remainder of the sentence is equally untrue."

got it blackened with printing ink, and exclaimed, " it is dirty
—very dirty—work!" The Fiscal very nearly got his hand
smashed by putting it on the "ribs " when the Irish pressman,
named Donovan, was rolling in the " coffin" (iron plate on which
the type is placed), and screamed out just in time to save his
hand, when Pat exclaimed, " Oh ! the darlint, she thinks your
Honour is going to print the *Facts !*" The Fiscal, now vexed,
said, " Have you no more presses ?" " No more printing
presses," replied Mr. Greig. " I think we should seal up the
types," continued the Fiscal. " Is it so stated in the warrant ?"
asked Mr. Greig. The Fiscal, pulling out the warrant, looked
at it, and said, " It is not so expressed." The Fiscal and his
followers were preparing to depart, when Mr. Greig requested
a copy of the warrant. " I am no copyist," said the Fiscal,
" *and my clerks do not work on Sundays.* To-morrow, perhaps,
you may have a copy." Mr. Greig remonstrated, stating that
his time was short to arrange his affairs. He wished to know
exactly what the Governor required of him, that he might
obey it to the letter, and requested to be allowed to copy it
himself. The Fiscal consented. Mr. Greig copied the
warrant (he was a very fast writer), and the Fiscal and his
followers departed, delighted that he had prevented the
publication of the *Facts* the following morning, as advertised
in the handbills. Vain thought ! The greater portion of
the *Facts* had already been put into type—the "warrant"
and the circumstances of that day were soon added ;
the operatives were at work (the writer amongst others)
during the whole of that Sunday night, and the following
morning, to the amazement of the Governor and the
Fiscal, hundreds of copies of the " *Facts connected with the
stoppage of the South African Commercial Advertiser,*" were
distributed gratis to the public. The street in front of the
office was filled with hundreds of people, the " Facts " were
thrown out of the upper-story windows, and there was quite a

E

scramble below to obtain copies. There had been no prohibition to publish the " *Facts*," simply an order to seal up the *Press* or *Presses*. There was but *one* Printing Press, and that had been securely sealed by the Fiscal. How then were the " Facts " printed ? Printers will understand how. The type having been " made up," and " locked up " in the " chases" on the " imposing stones "; the paper having been already " wetted," and ready for printing, was laid, sheet after sheet, upon the type, after being inked ; a printers' press-" blanket" was then laid upon the paper, and with " mallet and planer" the impression was produced as fast as three printers could do the work all night long. The following morning the Fiscal appeared again, with an order to seal up the " *Types*," and the doors of the composing rooms were sealed up. Too late ! The public were in possession of the " Facts," and the greatest excitement and consternation prevailed in Cape Town. No one knew what would come next. In Mr. Greig's Memorial to Earl Bathurst he states as follows :—

" Among numerous placards which followed the extinction of the press in South Africa, one of an atrocious character was *said* to have been posted in the Heerengracht (Dreyer's corner) charging the Governor and Dr. Barry* with an abominable crime. The large subscription raised, exceeding 25,000 rixdollars, to discover the author, tempted a servant of Mr. Edwards to accuse him and a Mr. Wilmot. In the course of the examination he introduced *my name* also : and a warrant was obtained for searching my premises for ' illegal documents.' My Lord, in adverting to this circumstance, I do it, not so much with a view to complain of the indignity of being compelled, upon a vague charge, to exhibit my most *private* papers and documents, but to show that I was throughout

* Dr. Barry will be remembered by some of the elder inhabitants of Cape Town. He was a small, delicate-looking person, without whiskers or beard. Report had it that he was a woman in disguise, which, it was said, was verified on his death. The writer remembers him (or her) well.

pursued with unremitting rancour and virulence, and after the *perjury* of the informer was thoroughly exposed, the Governor, although he had previously promised me copies of the depositions, refused to interfere, nor would the Fiscal prosecute the man for perjury."

The following extract of the ' Facts," in conclusion, is here copied :—

" Thus terminated," says the writer of the " Facts," " the *South African Commercial Advertiser*, in the eighteenth week of its existence, and such has been the fate of the first man who dared to express in print the obligations of Morality, the consolations and duties of Religion, and the principles of British Justice in this Colony. One circumstance more may be stated to illustrate the value of this newspaper. The Fiscal, in the month of February, instituted a prosecution against Messrs. Cooke, Edwards and Hoffman, for a Libel. Mr. Greig reported the proceedings of the Court, and these gentlemen were acquitted of all the charges brought against them. Shortly after the Fiscal again brought a criminal action against the same Edwards, for a Libel ; but to prevent interruption, put out, in the meantime, the candles of the Press, as has been before stated. Mr. Edwards was found guilty, *and sentenced to seven years' transportation without a single witness being called, or any other evidence considered besides the showing of the Fiscal.* The whole of this extensive, loyal and once promising Colony is thus laid prostrate at the feet of some dark inexplicable power—whose future who shall tell ? and under the operation and fear of which no industry can ensure success, nor any good design be prosecuted with confidence or safety."

The *South African Commercial Advertiser* having been suppressed, the second trial of the unfortunate William Edwards was never published. It did not suit the policy of the *South African Chronicle* to publish the proceedings. William Edwards was indicted for an alleged libel on the Governor, Lord Charles Somerset. A mock trial ensued, and he was sentenced to seven years' transportation, "without a single witness being called or any other evidence considered besides

E 2

the showing of the Fiscal." He was sent to prison, and steps taken for his immediate transportation. His sympathisers, however, made arrangements to effect his escape. Small files were introduced into his cell (on the upper story, facing the street), two iron bars were filed through, a rope ladder handed up to him at night, by which he descended, his trusty servant Thos. Mahony being in waiting below with a horse. What further happened is thus stated in the *South African Chronicle* of the 18th August, 1824 :—

' Orders having been received for the removal of William Edwards under sentence of transportation to New South Wales, to be placed on board the convict ship *Minerva*, in Simon's Bay, he was removed on the 17th September, 1824, in charge of the third Under-Sheriff Stilwell, and a constable, both on horseback. At the ' Three Cups,' Rondebosch, he feigned illness, and was permitted to leave the cart. On approaching Captain Carnall's place, near Wynberg, he was met by that gentleman on horseback, and was permitted, through indisposition, to proceed to Captain Carnall's house. Still ill, or pretending to be so, he retired to an inner room, leaving Stilwell on the outside. From this room he made his exit, and found a horse equipped and in waiting for him, and set off with all possible speed to Simon's Town. Stilwell at length got alarmed at the long absence of his prisoner, and finding him flown, and noticing the footprints of a horse, went in pursuit ; meeting Under-Sheriff Van der Schyff, who had seen Edwards on the road, both joined in pursuit. First they found Edwards' horse, entirely blown and unable to move. Edwards' footprints were traced to a rock at the edge of the sea, to give an idea that he had drowned himself. But Edwards had made his way back to Capt. Carnall's (taking off his boots whenever the ground would show his 'spoor'), where he arrived in the evening. He was, however, traced, and Capt. Carnall's house surrounded by Major Molesworth and some Dragoons, and some Military from Newlands. The premises were entered, and after considerable search Edwards was found concealed in his wife's bed-room, under the mattress, his wife being in bed. He was at once overpowered, but during the struggle contrived to inflict a superficial wound on his throat with a razor."

Captain Carnall and W. Stilwell were tried on the 27th September before two Commissioners of the Worshipful Court of Justice, and ultimately sentenced, Captain Carnall to one year's banishment from the Colony and to be placed on Robben Island until the sentence should be enforced. He was further fined Rds. 50 (£3 15s.) *for not proving his allegations*. W. Stilwell was sentenced to three months' imprisonment. Although the trial lasted many days, and much evidence was taken, no report appeared in the *South African Chronicle*, the Government organ.

"These occurrences," wrote Mr. Pringle, "produced a strong sensation in Cape Town. No public meeting could be held without the Governor's permission ; but a petition to the King in Council, praying for the extension to the Colony of the privileges of a Free Press, was drawn up, and signed by a very large proportion of the most respectable inhabitants, including almost the whole of the English merchants. This petition was couched in the most moderate and decorous language, and only referred in very calm and measured terms to the recent extraordinary transactions. Such was the *panic*, however, that had been excited by the sentence of banishment issued against Mr. Greig, that comparatively few of the Dutch inhabitants dared to sign it. The Governor's power, they said ' was absolute ' and his resentment ' ruin.' They durst not venture, even to petition the King contrary to the pleasure of the Governor. Such abject dread of arbitrary power found little sympathy, of course, in our breasts. Mr. Fairbairn and I signed the petition."

Not satisfied with stopping the Press, and issuing a sentence of *banishment from the Colony* against its proprietor, the Governor next turned his vindictive feelings against Messrs. Pringle and Fairbairn. "From that moment," says Mr. Pringle, "the prosperity of our Academy was blasted. Week after week pupils were taken away, some on one pretext, some on another; until, in the course of a few months, scarcely half our former number remained.'' This result was probably accelerated by certain occurrences which took place shortly after the affair of the Press, and of which the following is not the least memorable and characteristic :—

"The establishment of a Literary and Scientific Society at the Cape had been one of the objects to which we had most earnestly directed our attention, with the view to the intellectual improvement of the Colony ; and in order to prepare the public mind for the formation of such an association, two able articles from the pen of Mr. Fairbairn had appeared in successive numbers of our *Magazine*. After the suppression of the Press, we still cherished the hope of succeeding in this object, which had now become of more importance than ever, since by that event 'light' was 'by one entrance quite shut out.' Besides, as such societies have been generally tolerated, and even liberally patronized, by some of the most despotic Governments of ancient and modern times, we flattered ourselves that even our South African 'divan' would be disposed rather to encourage than obstruct the direction of the public mind to such pursuits, both for the sake of their own credit in the eyes of the Commissioners and the Home Government, and in order to withdraw attention from more unpleasant topics.

"On the 11th July, accordingly, we met with a few of our friends at the house of Messrs. Thomson and Pillans, merchants in Cape Town, to concert measures for carrying this purpose into effect. Some fundamental resolutions were adopted ; a committee of three persons was appointed to prepare specific regulations, &c. Copies of these regulations, &c., were transmitted to the Colonial Office, the Fiscal, the members of the Court of Justice, and to the Commissioners of Inquiry. The members at this time had increased to 61, comprising among others the Chief Justice, and two other members of the Bench, the Deputy Fiscal, Mr. Lind, four other civil servants, two advocates, four ministers of religion nine medical gentlemen, and twenty-one merchants. A deputation, consisting of the Chief Justice, Sir John Truter, Dr. Truter, a member of the Bench (and brother-in-law of Mr. Barrow, of the Admiralty) Mr. Advocate Cloete, two Indian residents, two medical gentlemen, and two English merchants of Cape Town."

" The Governor, however," wrote Mr. Pringle, " did not allow time for the deputation to wait upon him. He had been watching our proceedings all along, with a most feline vigilance, and now sprung forth upon us like a tiger from his den. He called the Chief Justice to his presence, and gave him such a rating for joining the Society, that Sir John, almost frightened out of his wits, anxiously entreated me to withdraw his name from the list of members ; at the same time assuring me, with a sort of rueful simplicity, that he conscientiously believed the institution to be a most praiseworthy one, and calculated to be of inestimable advantage to the community ! ! !

" With Mr. Advocate Cloete his Lordship came at once to the point, and told him distinctly that he was resolved to crush the institution ; adding, with vindictive emphasis, that it was quite sufficient for him to know that the Society had originated with Mr. Pringle and Mr. Fairbairn—for he was fully determined, so long as he held the reins of Government, to oppose and thwart *everything*, without exception, which emanated from them, or in which they were concerned."

What a Governor ! What a Chief Justice ! ! And this during the lifetime of several persons still living !

Mr. Greig had made arrangements for leaving the Colony, and had advertised a Public Sale of his effects for Monday, the 24th May, when late on *Sunday* evening, the 23rd, he received from His Majesty's Fiscal the following note :—

"Cape Town, May 23, 1824.

" To Mr. George Greig,—Sir,—Considering that the advertisement in the Cape *Gazette* of yesterday, for the disposal of your

effects to-morrow, had relation to the order I communicated to you
on the 9th instant, to quit the Colony in a month from that period;
and being aware that it had not been His Excellency the Governor's
intention to enforce that order, unless some fresh cause for its
necessity should arise, I have obtained His Excellency's permission
to inform you, that His Excellency has been pleased to rescind that
order, and to signify his permission for you to remain in the
Colony.

"I am, &c.,

"(Signed) D. Denyssen, Fiscal."

To which Mr. Greig returned the following reply :—

"Cape Town, May 25, 1824.

"Sir,—I received your note of Sunday last, May 23, signifying
your having obtained His Excellency's permission to communicate
to me that it was not His Excellency's intention to enforce the order
respecting my expulsion from this Colony, unless I should com-
mit some fault or other tending to render such a measure necessary.
I beg to state, in return, that, in consequence of His Excellency's
order, my flourishing trade has been ruined,—my honourable prospects of usefulness for the present destroyed,—my character as a
man and a subject defamed,—my friends alarmed and shaken, —my
people scattered, and exposed to poverty and starvation, on account
of their having accepted employment from me. In consequence of
that order, also, I have made my arrangements for quitting the
Colony. I have written to England to retain Counsel for the re-
covery of damages adequate to my enormous losses; and to get the
stamp of *sedition* taken off my character by the proper authorities.
I cannot, therefore, in conscience, say that I feel in any way
relieved by your communication, in which I see nothing of
remuneration, or my being restored to the situation in which I was
placed before I was assailed by the Government.

"I am, &c.,

"(Signed) George Greig."

"D. Denyssen, Esq., H.M. Fiscal."

Mr. Greig accordingly proceeded to England within the time ordered, and was successsful in obtaining justice from. the Imperial Government. He returned to the Colony, and by order of Earl Bathurst, Secretary of State for the Colonies, his Press was relieved from censorship, and written authority was given that he should not be further interfered with, and the publication of the *South African Commercial Advertiser* was resumed under the sole management of Mr. John Fairbairn. Lord Charles Somerset was at once recalled to vindicate himself against the charges brought against his administration. He never returned to the Colony, and was succeeded on the 8th February, 1826, by Lieut.-Governor Richard Bourke, who again in September, 1828, was succeeded by Sir Lowry Cole. But while in England Lord Charles Somerset, by his family and other influence, succeeded in procuring an order from Downing-street for the suppression of the *South African Commercial Advertiser* for the second time, which order reached the Colony in 1827. The ground alleged for this act was not the publication of any obnoxious original article, but an extract copied from the London *Times* of January 25, 1826. Mr. John Fairbairn was hereupon sent to England as a delegate from the Cape public, and on his arrival in England was supported by the influence of the merchants and others connected with the Colony. A change of Ministry had also taken place, and the new Secretary of State for the Colonies, Mr. Huskisson, conceded to the expressed wishes of the colonists, and intimated on behalf of the Government that "the Press would be placed under the control and protection of *the Law*, and that no arbitrary suppression should take place in future." Mr. Fairbairn returned to the Colony triumphantly, and the South African Press has been FREE ever since.

———

It may be as well here to state that immediately after Mr. Greig left the Colony, in accordance with the order of Lord

Charles Somerset, his (Greig's) press and printing materials came
into the possession of Mr. William Bridekirk (nephew to the
then Port Captain, Captain Bridekirk). Mr. William Bridekirk was at the time a compositor in the Government Printing
Office, where the Cape *Gazette* was printed. Mr. Bridekirk at
once started a weekly newspaper, called the *South African
Chronicle*, and had the assistance of several of the compositors
of the Government Printing Office. Not wishing his son to
lose what he had learnt in Mr. Greig's establishment, the
writer's father agreed, on the solicitation of Mr. Bridekirk, that
his son should enter Mr. Bridekirk's establishment, with the
understanding that should Mr. Greig return to the Colony, he
(the writer) would be permitted again to join Mr. Greig's
establishment. This was accordingly done, and on the return
of Mr. Greig, the writer went back and remained until he
finally left Cape Town for the frontier about the middle of the
year, 1828. Soon after Mr. Greig's return the *South African
Chronicle* ceased to exist.* Other newspapers were also started,
such as the *Zuid-Afrikaan*; the *Colonist*, by Mr. W. Beddy,
M A., Trinity College, Dublin (afterwards Clerk to the Clerk

---

* A remarkable circumstance happened to the writer. He had been in
the habit of ' composing" (setting up into type) the leading articles of the
South African Chronicle, and was inquisitive to know the name of the
Editor, but could not find out. One night he dreamt that a gentleman
had come into the printing office, and handed " copy ' of the leading article
to him. He took particular notice of the gentleman's features, and not
long afterwards came across a gentleman in the streets whose features he at
once recognized as the person he had seen in his dream. A few days
subsequently he had to take a note to the Public Library, then held in
the Exchange, and saw the identical face. Struck with the likeness, he
made inquiries, and found it was Mr. A. J. Jardine, Librarian, and, under
the rose, Editor of the *South African Chronicle* He had never seen Mr.
Jardine before until he met him in the street, after his dream. The
Chronicle was "inspired" by the Government.

of the Peace, Graham's Town; the *Verzamelaar*, by J. Suasso de Lima, &c.*

° Mr. J. Suasso de Lima was a Dutch lawyer, a clever man, and a linguist. He was always in trouble; never paid anybody, especially his house-rent. On one occasion he had to change his residence, but there was a writ of "gyseling" (civil imprisonment) out against him, and constables on the watch. To effect his removal he obtained a large "ballast-mant" (clothes basket), got into it, and had it covered over with books, newspapers, &c, and carried by two "coolies." The constables on the watch being suspicious, gave chase; the frightened "coolies" abandoned their charge, the basket upset, and De Lima rolled out. Mr. De Lima was caught, and paid the writ. When he started the *Verzamelaar* (Gleaner), as was the custom with printers, the "formes," or type, of the first number had to be "christened" by the overseer of the office by spilling some wine over the type, while the printers had each to drink a glass to the success of the new infant. Mr. De Lima was lame (one leg shorter than the other), and generally wore a long grey overcoat, with a large pocket on each side. The usual warrant of "gyseling" was out against him. The writer accompanied him towards evening to fetch the wine. Mr. De. L. put a bottle into each pocket, and when near the office, the constables gave chase—a run had to be made— the bottles clashed—and broke—but the Editor got safely into the office. The *Verzamelaar* was a kind of Dutch *Punch*, and the editor was constantly in hot water for his personalities. There was a Dutch Doctor V. H. in Cape Town very much smitten with a handsome young lady, Miss A. M. Escorting her home one night from a party just at midnight—arriving before the door of her mother's house, a cock crew —Dr. V. H. made a pun—

> De haan kraait koeker-de-koe,
> De deur is toe.

The lady of the house, who was not favourable to the doctor, at that moment opened the door, and replied

> Neen, Mynheer! de deur is open,
> En gy kunt naar den drommel loopen.

The next morning the impromptu verses were in the *Verzamelaar*, and poor De Lima threatened with a horsewhipping from the irate doctor.

PART II.

The Establishment of the Eastern Province Press.

COME we now to the establishment of the first newspaper in the Eastern Province, viz., *The Graham's Town Journal.*

As already stated, among the British Settlers who arrived in Table Bay in 1820, were Messrs. Robert Godlonton and Thomas Stringfellow. Both these gentlemen were practical printers, and had, before leaving England, been engaged in a branch of the King's Printing Office, at Shacklewell, and the manager of the establishment, Mr. Rutt, anxious to give them a fair start, had consigned to them the whole plant of a printing establishment, in conjunction with Dr. Roberts, afterwards a medical practitioner in Cape Town, with the distinct understanding that if they were successful, he should be paid for his venture; and if not, no demand would be made upon them on account of it. "On our arrival in Table Bay," wrote Mr. Godlonton, "it soon became known that a Printing Press was among the emigrants' luggage, and the Government printer, Mr. Van de Sandt, was sent on board to make the inquiry. The result was a prohibition against its going any further, the Acting Governor (Lieut.-General Donkin) remarking, as we were told, that to allow it to go forward would be equal to scattering firebrands along the Eastern frontier. We were under quarantine at the time, not that any sickness was on board, but to prevent the emigrants from going ashore, and falling in love with Cape Town. But, notwithstanding this, for the purpose of carrying out the arrangements of the Government, Mr.

Stringfellow, was permitted to go on shore, and between him
and the Government printer the matter was finally settled.
The amount of the invoice was paid, and remitted by Dr.
Roberts to Mr. Rutt, in England. By a curious chain of
circumstances *this identical press* came into my possession at
Graham's Town, and was used in printing the first newspaper
ever published in the Eastern Province. A portion of the
' platen ' now stands as a memorial on my library table."

The manner in which the *identical press* brought out by
Messrs. Stringfellow and Godlonton (an old-style wooden press)
afterwards came into the possession of the latter gentleman is
remarkable. It has already been stated that the writer of these
" Reminiscences " had been taught the art of printing in Mr.
Geo. Greig's establishment in Cape Town. Printers in those
days were not to be had in the Colony. Not only was the
writer engaged in the mechanical part of printing the *South
African Commercial Advertiser*, but he also became proof-reader
to both Messrs. Fairbairn and Pringle. In 1828, having lost his
only surviving parent, the writer proceeded to Graaff-Reinet with
a friend, from whence he went across the Orange River (then a
wild country, uninhabited except by wandering Bushmen) with
a shooting party of Dutch farmers. Graaff-Reinet at that
period was an " oasis in the desert," the farmers travelling to
Cape Town in ox-wagons, with their butter, fat and skins.
Woolled sheep had not yet been introduced. Returning to
Graaff-Reinet after some months' absence, the writer ascertained that the press and printing plant taken from Messrs.
Stringfellow and Godlonton had, to get it out of harm's way,
been transferred to Graaff-Reinet, where an amateur printer,
the late Mr. P. C. Wahlstrand, was employed in printing
Government forms for the use of the public offices, the salary of
the printer amounting to more than the "forms" were worth.

The " Freedom of the Press " having been obtained, there
was no longer any fear of the " Settlers' Press " getting into

other hands. It was sold by public auction, at Graaff-Reinet, and bought by the writer. Following the advice of several friends, the writer took his press and plant to Graham's Town, where he commenced a printing establishment in the month of September, 1830. The British Settlers were not a people to have a printing press in their midst, and not to have a newspaper of their own. Messrs. Godlonton and Stringfellow were then residing in Graham's Town, both being in the Civil Service.

The writer was soon solicited to establish a newspaper, but there was an unforeseen difficulty. A stringent law was in existence regulating the printing of newspapers, the preamble of which was as follows :—"Ordinance for preventing the *mischiefs* arising from the printing and publishing newspapers, and papers of a like nature, by persons not known, and for regulating the printing and publication of such papers in other respects ; and also for restraining the abuses arising from the publication of blasphemous and seditious libels." One of the provisions of this Ordinance was, that "no person shall print or publish within the Colony of the Cape of Good Hope, or any of the dependencies thereof, any newspaper, or any such paper as aforesaid, until an affidavit or affidavits, affirmation or affirmations made and signed as hereinafter mentioned, and containing the several matters and things hereinafter for that purpose specified and mentioned, shall have been delivered to the Colonial Secretary, or Acting Colonial Secretary, *at his office*" (in Cape Town). The affidavits were to be made in writing, *before the Colonial Secretary,* 600 miles from Graham's Town *;* and the printer or publisher to enter into Security Bonds in the sum of £300, and two or three sureties in like sum, in the event of any judgment being given against printer, editor, or publisher, for printing or publishing any blasphemous or seditious libel. Before the writer, therefore, could establish his projected newspaper—the *Graham's Town Journal*—he had to proceed to Cape Town, a distance of 600 miles. Travelling then was very different from what it is now; there were no passenger or mail carts—indeed there were no carts at all—the mails from and to Cape Town, &c., were carried on horseback in huge leather bags, heavy enough to break the back of the unfortunate animal which carried them. Then it involved a journey on horseback to Port Elizabeth, about 75 miles, and a sea voyage thence to Table Bay in a small coasting schooner of 80 tons,* in which the "bilge-water," as it was called, was enough to stifle one. Having arrived in Cape Town, the writer had to procure a certificate—which he was fortunately able to do—that he was worth £300, before he was allowed to enter into a Surety Bond before the Colonial Secretary; then he had to find three sureties (who had to procure similar certificates). The following are copies from the originals, now filed among the archives in the Colonial Office :—

I, the undersigned, Louis Henry Meurant, do hereby declare and make oath, that I, living at Graham's Town, am the editor of a certain newspaper to be entitled the *Graham's Town Journal*, and that I am also the proprietor of the said newspaper, and further that I am the printer and publisher of the said paper, at Graham's Town.

Cape Town, 22nd November, 1831.

(Signed)   L. H. MEURANT.

Sworn before me, Colonial Office, Cape Town, Cape of Good Hope, this 22nd day of November, 1831.

(Signed)   JOHN BELL, Sec. to Government.

* On one occasion the writer had to proceed from Port Elizabeth to Table Bay in a 30 ton cutter, the crew consisting of Captain, cook and a boy. The voyage occupied three weeks. The poor little craft afterwards made one voyage too many, and went down " with all hands."

I, the undersigned, do hereby certify that Louis Henry Meurant, printer, in Graham's Town, has duly entered into a recognizance on the 21st day of October last, before the Honourable Mr. Justice Menzies, whereby he bound himself in the sum of £300, and three sureties in the sum of £100 each, as editor, printer and publisher of a newspaper to be entitled *The Graham's Town Journal*.

Cape Town, 22nd November, 1831.

WALT. HARDING, Acting Registrar of Court.

(Signed)   T. H. BOWLES,
Registrar of the Supreme Court.

But this was not all. He had to lay in a supply of paper for twelve months, and to have every sheet stamped with a penny stamp at the Stamp Office, in Cape Town, and which had to be paid for in cash.

Graham's Town was not the City then which it is now. As Mrs. Malaprop would have said, it was then in a state of "infanticide" (infancy). There were some amusing stories told of its "infanticide" days. A Mr. Kromhout was the Field-cornet, and auctioneer, and jack-of-all-trades. In ringing his brass plate at the commencement of a sale his stereotyped condition was—" drie monts krediet for de Christemens—no krediet for de Settlaar." The latter term was then, and for some years afterwards, one of opprobrium. Mr. Kromhout had a colleague, who generally assisted him in holding inquests, valuing damages to gardens, &c.; this gentleman went by the name of Peculiar Clarke. He dropped his *h's*, and laid great stress on his *v's*. and *w's*. Major Dundas was the Landdrost. On one occasion Messrs. Kromhout and *Peculiar* Clarke had to hold an inquest, on returning from which they had to report the appearances of the body to the Landdrost. Mr. Peculiar Clarke reported " that when they came to the body " the *wital* spark was quite extinc*k*." " Yes, Meneer," chimed in Kromhout, " he *stink* very mosh."

The Rev. H. Dugmore, in his "Reminiscences of an Albany Settler," also tells some amusing stories. Take the following:—"One of our old Queen's Town Field-cornets, in the days of his youth, took charge of the party's ration sheep (the Settlers were located in parties) from Bathurst to Green Fountain. The sheep numbered probably twelve to fifteen. Those who know that part of the country know what an excellent field it is for a sheep chase; and how a dozen of startled hamels, just separated from a large flock, would be likely to try a driver's legs, and lungs, too, in crossing it. If the course of the journey could have been afterwards traced on a chart it would have looked like the working out of some intricate geometrical problem. Such a succession of zig-zags, angles, and arcs of circles, no ship, beating up against contrary winds, ever described. To mend matters, after miles of open plain had been traversed, there lay a tract of 'enchanted ground' in the shape of a belt of thick mimosa woodland, right across the way home. By dint of unconquerable perseverance the sheep were brought thus far; and then! one starting this way, two in that, three in the other; a rent in the coat in stopping these; face scratched and eyes endangered in turning those; a shout to his two companions to ascertain where the rest were; an impenetrable barrier of bush stopping all access to them. Before giving up all for lost our friend declared he had run the sheep so hard, though they had large tails at starting, they had melted away to half the size by the time he had done with them! Driven to desperation he at length exclaimed:—'Dead or alive I'll secure *one* of you at any rate,' as a discharge from his fowling-piece stretched it on the ground before him. But he was still miles away from home. Of his two companions one *couldn't* and the other *wouldn't* take his share in carrying the dead sheep. There was nothing left for it but to shoulder it himself; and sturdy John Staples showed that if his own staple was not very *long* it was very good, for

F

carried his load *home*. It was the only sheep of the lot that reached its intended destination—the wild dogs, wolves and jackals got all the rest."

Take another instance of how far the Settlers were fitted for the work of bringing the wilderness into cultivation. Some sowed carrot seed at the bottom of trenches two spades deep, filling up the trenches with soil as soon as it was done. The remark of one who saw them was, "It will come up most likely in England about the time it does here." In another case a man wishing to get some mealies for seed, applied to his neighbour who had obtained a supply just before, but found he had planted the whole, without knocking it off the cobs! A third person planted out a lot of young onions, "roots upwards."

There is another good story told, which has been extracted from the *Graham's Town Journal*, for which the writer remembers the late Mr. Webb (better known in Graham's Town as *Doctor* Webb), painter and glazier, was responsible :—

A Settler, of the name of H., head of a small party near Bathurst, went one day (no great while after locating) to Capt. T., then acting Landdrost at Bathurst, to have some advice about his land. After obtaining the information wanted, he abruptly exclaimed—" I don't know if it is worth while to bother myself about the land, as most likely I shall not be permitted to hold it." "Not hold it ?" exclaimed the Captain, "why not, Mr. H. ?" "Why Sir, in the Government Circular, with which we were furnished in England, there is some reservation mentioned." "Reservation ! Mr. H.," said the Captain with an air of curiosity. "What reservation ?" "Why, such as mines of *precious stones*, Sir." "What, said he eagerly, have you any such things on your location ?" "Yes, Sir, I have." The Captain (now all politeness): "Take a chair, Mr. H., sit down." (Being seated.) What kind of precious stones ?" " *Precious big ones*, Sir," said the wag, and retired in haste.

The ground which is now adorned by splendid edifices was

crossed by footpaths. The public offices were in a barn, where the Circuit Courts were also held. Judges wore wigs, and the " bar " was represented by " agents." On one occasion, a Hottentot being on his trial, was asked by the interpreter whether he had any objection to any of the jury who were about to " sit " on his case. Scanning the jurymen for some minutes attentively, and then looking up at the Judge, he replied, " No objection to those ' baase,' I object to the baas with the *witkop* (wig). I want him to leave the Court." ·

Mais revenon a nos moutons.—The day was at length fixed for the publication of the first number of the *Graham's Town Journal*. The young " Settler " was to be introduced into life with a flourish of trumpets, and half-a-dozen " Prospectuses " were forwarded to the writer, one of them more especially, most grandiloquent. The author is now no more, and for obvious reasons his name is not mentioned. The following is a copy :—

" TO THE PUBLIC,

" Respectfully soliciting their co-operation in establishing a Weekly Paper, to be printed in English only, at Graham's Town, and to be called *The Albanian*, or *Eastern Province Register*.

" Near eighteen eventful months have vanished since the necessity of introducing some check upon the arbitrary dissemination of one set of principles was acknowledged by many inhabitants of the Colony; and to place the feeling then manifested beyond the chance of reasonable contravention, it is sufficient to observe that the *Zuid-Afrikaan* at one period could boast of having 700 subscribers.

" We were not then prepared for entering the Lists, to maintain the independent designation of Eastern Provincials ; but the time appears to have arrived—a PRESS is now in Albany, and if we are ripe for, and really wish a Representative Assembly, there must be intellect enough amongst us to keep step in the universal march. ' Nothing venture, nothing have,' as Poor Richard says. Let us muster our forces. From the Western Districts (not excluding Cape

Town) good wishes and assistance is to be hoped for ; these, with
the Commercial Mart of Graham's Town, daily improving,—the
rising Port of Algoa Bay, in the populous district of Uitenhage,—
the unobtrusive people of George,—the hoarded news from Graaff-
Reinet, which, whilome, through the medium of the *Commercial
Advertiser*, shone forth a brilliant example to all around ;—Beaufort
also—and the good folks of Somerset united ; surely with these,
and when other resources, to be named hereafter, are brought into
operation, we can furnish such a sufficient support to a Paper as
shall indicate the political distinction conferred by the wisdom of
His Majesty's Commissioners of Inquiry. Without a union of this
kind, the distinction is, in our opinion, a nonentity.

"Having beat a roll-call, instead of sounding pibrochs of Gathering,
it remains for you, Most Potential Public, to fall into our ranks,—
set the Artillery of the Provincial Press in motion, under the motto
of ' OPEN TO ALL PARTIES, INFLUENCED BY NONE "; our Marching
Order will then be complete ; and we shall steadily advance
towards the attainment of the Glorious, the Just Privilege of
Legislating for Ourselves.

"Be contented to consider our first efforts at skirmishing—
' Rome was not built in a day '; so do not be discouraged should
we not dash on with sparkling Literary Abilities ; Shakespeare's
advice to Lovers when they are at a loss for lack of matter, is, as
the cleanliest shift, to KISS ; we, as general Lovers of the Colony,
follow the hint, and WRITE ; trusting to get method and wisdom as
we go on. Without auxiliaries, however, we are nothing, and we
earnestly call on every person in the Eastern and Western districts,
who has the welfare of his Fellow Creatures at heart, to aid us with
Communications, and even Gleanings on all subjects of general or
local import. Those from Cape Town will be highly valuable, as
the greatest difficulty under which we shall labour must arise from
not having immediate access to the English Papers. It shall be our
endeavour to make up for this considerable deficiency, by carefully
selecting any novelties that may have been omitted in the other
periodicals; and as it is likely to be our lot to differ from the political
conclusions formed by the editors of those, it shall not be for want

of assiduity if we do not produce some new feature. On the other hand, we hope to have the earliest and most copious intelligence from the interior; the market prices of the Frontier Districts are to be inserted in turn, so as for one to appear each week. We propose procuring reports from the various Magistrates' Courts; observations of interest; accounts of school progress; public meetings; shipping news; christenings, marriages, &c., &c., &c., will be thankfully received; and as this intercommunication between the East and West will facilitate commercial and other intercourse, the advantage of advertising in our columns cannot fail suggesting itself in numerous instances.

"All the foregoing, and as much more as we are able to perform, will be forwarded to every part of the Colony at Rds. 16 per annum, or Rds. 4 per quarter (including stamps and postage), and in Town at Rds. 13 per annum, or Rds. 3.2 per quarter; and when our List of Subscribers shall contain 250 names, the first number of *The Albanian*, or *Eastern Province Register*, will be immediately struck off, of which timely notice will be given to our Subscribers, to enable them to forward their communications.

"To be paid on delivery of the first number, and afterwards for every quarter in advance.

"Subscription Lists lie open for Signature at the Stores of Mr. B. Norden, and Messrs. P. Heugh & Co., Graham's Town."

At length the name *Graham's Town Journal* was adopted, and the following, written by the late Lieut. T. C. White, of Table Farm, near Graham's Town, to whose memory belongs the honour of having introduced the infant paper, for infant it was in size as well as pretension: —

"In presenting to the public the first number of the *Graham's Town Journal*, the proprietor feels it necessary that he should offer a concise view of the motives, objects and proposed scope of his undertaking.

"The importance of Graham's Town as a commercial station alone seems sufficient to entitle it to a local newspaper; or, in other words, appears to ensure adequate remuneration to the proprietor.

" It must, indeed, be matter of surprise that a newspaper has so long been dispensed with by a community distinguished for its activity, intelligence and enterprise. At a distance of 600 miles from the seat of Government and Press, upon a soil and under a climate in many respects dissimilar from those of the Western districts of the Colony, with the opposition of interests and the diversity of opinions which must necessarily have existed, there could have been no deficiency of matter for profitable discussion ; and as even such objects as are common to both extremities of the Colony, when observed from different points of view and in different lights, frequently present a considerable change in their features and characteristics, the proprietor, by opening a channel for conveying to Government and the public the opinions of the Eastern districts upon matters of general as well as local interest, would have had some claim to support on the ground of general utility.

" But independent of these considerations the proprietor of the *Graham's Town Journal* is led to expect that the commercial and other interests of Albany will afford sufficient matter for support of his paper. Its chief town has risen into an importance second to Cape Town only ; its exports and imports approach two millions of rixdollars annually ; its traffic with the tribes in the interior is boundless in its extent, and promises to afford ample employment to an increased population and an enlarged capital ; and the direct trade to England has been established on a permanent basis. In this stage of their prosperity the inhabitants of Albany have consented to indulge in the luxury of a newspaper. This consent has been signified to the proprietor by a respectable body of subscribers in Albany, Cape Town, and other parts of the Colony, and this expression of the public will has been the proprietor's chief motive for establishing the paper.

" One grand object of the proprietor of any newspaper, under whatever figure of speech the *generous* public may be apostrophized, must be to make his speculation *pay ;* which end can only be obtained by giving satisfaction to the public. The proprietor will therefore confine himself to stating the means he proposes to employ for the attainment of that object.

"Local Intelligence of Public Interest, connected with the Commerce and Agriculture of the Frontier ; information respecting the condition of the neighbouring tribes ; selections from the English and other newspapers, from periodicals and other interesting publications ; reports of law proceedings ; the state of the markets ; together with the communications of correspondents, and the advertisements with which he may be favoured, are all the proprietor can offer for the present.

"Correspondents may depend upon the secrecy and honour of the editor, and the public may rely upon a rigid exercise of the editorial prerogative of rejection, should anything be offered unfit for the public eye, whether arising from the matter or manner of the communication ; and this right he feels will be the more readily acquiesced in, as the editor will carefully abstain from taking any part in the discussions in which his correspondents may be engaged.

"The editor does not propose to inflict *iuvariably* on his readers what is usually called a LEADING ARTICLE. Perhaps he has not yet chosen a political hobby horse, and is not prepared to witch the world with didactic essays. Be this as it may, the proprietor confidently hopes that his humble undertaking will prove serviceable to the public, even if it should do no more than afford a ready and convenient means of circulating advertisements and of communicating commercial and other useful information."

Thus, then, was the first number of the *Graham's Town Journal*—the first newspaper printed out of Cape Town, in the "City of the Settlers"—ushered into life, on Friday, the 30th December, 1831. Small as the paper was (half sheet double crown) it was no small matter to get it printed. Printers there were none. The proprietor had to teach apprentices, and to do much of the mechanical part himself. The press was an old wooden one ; there were no " composition " rollers or balls, and steam was not dreamt of.

The editor, printer, publisher and proprietor were all combined in one person, a young man, a little over 20 years of age, who was somewhat in the same predicament as an American editor, who published the following notice :—" The editor, printer, publisher, foreman and eldest apprentice (*two* in all) are confined by sickness, and *the whole establishment* is left in the care of the *devil*."

The appearance of the first number of the *Graham's Town Journal* was a red-letter day in the Town (now City), after which it was named. Early on the morning of publication the street in front of the little office was crowded with anxious persons, jostling each other who should get the first paper. The arrival of the English Mail now-a-days with important news could not excite greater interest than was shown in Graham's Town on the 30th December, 1831. From that day the paper prospered. The prospectus contained in the first number was strictly carried out. There were no Editorial "Leading Articles"— Politics were left to be discussed by correspondents. It comprised The News of the Day,—Reports of Courts of Justice,— Extracts from English and Cape Town Newspapers,—and useful information on various subjects. The contributors were numerous, principally in " Original Correspondence," which formed the staple of the paper, and extracts from interesting works, &c. So well was the undertaking supported, that in about six months the proprietor had to enlarge its size to a full sheet of demy.

And here the writer of these Reminiscences wishes to correct an error into which several persons have fallen. In the " Story of the Settlement," published in Graham's Town, there is a reference to the first South African Newspaper, the *Commercial Advertiser*, and the paragraph concludes thus : "It will not be without interest, in this connection, if we here state, that this very press was brought to the Colony by Mr. Godlonton, but was confiscated on its arrival in Cape Town."

The *Graaff-Reinet Herald* of April 30, 1884, took up the subject, and said—" And also we were not aware that *the same press* happens to be in *our* possession, as we had no information that

Fairbairn's press and that of Mr. Godlonton were one and the same. There were among the British Settlers only four printers, namely,—Robert Godlonton, Wm. Cook, Thomas String-fellow, and another.* It was not till many years after his arrival that Mr. Godlonton resumed his trade in Graham's Town, and became proprietor of the *Graham's Town Journal*, some time after its establishment by Mr. L. H. Meurant, in 1832. We have no information how Mr. Fairbairn and Mr. Greig became possessed of the original press, which Mr· Godlonton landed at Cape Town. It has, however, been in Graaff-Reinet nearly 40 years to our knowledge. It is at present in our office, and daily doing serviceable work; and upon this now historical press, the first *Graaff-Reinet Herald* was first printed in 1852. It is a 'Stanhope,' of good work-manship, bearing engraved on its side 'Walker *fecit* No. 98.' "

There is a confusion in all these statements, which it is as well should be corrected. Mr. George Greig, as before stated, arrived in Cape Town from England not many months before he started the *South African Commercial Advertiser*, bringing with him the necessary plant for a printing office. The Rev· Dr. Philip, Superintendent of the London Missionary Society, had a *wooden* printing press, which he lent to Mr. Greig, until his own press should arrive, and which was the press sealed up by Lord Charles Somerset. Mr. Fairbairn had nothing what-ever to do with the "plant"; he did not become "possessed of the original press." He merely became joint editor with the late Thos. Pringle, as stated in Part I. of these " Remi-niscences." He had no property in the paper. When the *South African Commercial Advertiser* was suppressed in 1824, Dr. Philip's *wooden* press (formerly used by Mr. Greig) and Mr. Greig's type passed into the possession of Mr. William Bridekirk,

* The writer can supply the name of that other, viz.: - Samuel Mollett, whom he well knew as overseer in Mr. W. Bridekirk's printing office.

then a compositor in the Government Printing Office,* and
who then, August 18, 1824, started the *South African Chronicle*,
which was edited by Mr. A. J. Jardine, Librarian of the Cape
Town Public Library. There can be no doubt that the
Chronicle was a Government undertaking, and the articles which
appeared in it were inspired by Government officials and
toadies. It bore the " imprint " W. Bridekirk, editor, but Mr.
Jardine was the editor. Having failed to induce Mr. Greig to
remain in the Colony after his sentence of banishment, the
next best thing was to start a Government organ to endeavour
to counteract the feeling raised by the despotic conduct of the
Governor.

But to return from this digression. Mr. Greig's press,
as has been stated, was a *wooden* press (Mr. Philip's), and
passed into the possession of Mr. W. Bridekirk, in whose
printing office it still was when the writer left Cape Town for
Graaff-Reinet in the middle of 1828. Messrs. Godlonton and
Stringfellow's *wooden press* was sent to Graaff-Reinet shortly
after it was taken from those gentlemen ; and, as before stated,
the writer bought it from the Government in 1830, and took it
to Graham's Town, and from him it passed into the possession
of Mr. Godlonton, by sale, in 1839, when the partnership of
Meurant and Godlonton ceased by effluxion of time. That it

---

* Copy of a letter from Mr. George Greig to Earl Bathurst :—

" 32, City Road, 19th Nov , 1824.

"My Lord,—Having by late letters from the Cape of Good Hope
learned that a newspaper and printing establishment is commenced there
by a person formerly connected with the Colonial Printing Office, and
being aware that there were at the time no printing materials in the
Colony but those purchased from me and their own, I beg to inform your
Lordship of this fact, conceiving, as I do, that it adds an aggravating
ingredient to my case. Begging respectfully to solicit your Lordship's
early consideration to my case,

" I have, &c.,

" (Signed)   GEORGE GREIG."

was the identical press brought out by the Settlers the writer had from Mr. W. C. van Ryneveld, Civil Commissioner of Graaff-Reinet, and also from Mr. P. C. Wahlstrand, the Government printer. Besides this, not only the press but the type also were recognized by Messrs. Godlonton and Stringfellow on the arrival of the writer at Graham's Town. Surely no one will doubt all this testimony. But there *was* an old iron "Stanhope" press in the Government Printing Office, precisely such a one as the *Graaff-Reinet Herald* mentions, and it is not unlikely that it may have found its way to Graaff-Reinet. One thing, however, is certain, the *Graaff-Reinet Herald* was not printed on the Settlers' press in 1852, since that became the property of the writer in 1830 and was sold by him to Mr. Godlonton in 1839, and never passed out of the possession of the latter since.

Coming back from this digression it will not be out of place to record, for future reference, how the Settlers' press, as it may be called, again fell into the hands of one of its former proprietors, Mr. Godlonton.

When the *Graham's Town Journal* was started by the writer of these "Reminiscences," Mr. Godlonton was Chief Clerk in the office of the Civil Commissioner of Albany, Captain Duncan Campbell. Leading articles, as will be seen from the prospectus, were dispensed with, so that no "leader" writer was necessary. The custom at that time was that the Chief Clerk of the Civil Commissioner travelled annually in an ox-wagon to collect the "opgaaf" (taxes). Albany and Somerset were then one fiscal district, and this collecting journey took up several months. On Mr. Godlonton's return from one of these collecting journeys in May, 1832, he wrote an account of the Kat River Settlement, then newly formed, which appeared in the *Graham's Town Journal*, No. 24, of the 8th June, 1832, under the signature of R. G. This was Mr. Godlonton's *first* contribution to the *Journal*. The subject

being interesting, even at this distance of time, a few extracts
are here inserted :—

"The population of the Settlement may be estimated at 1,500
inhabitants, consisting of Bastards and Hottentots, natives of the
countries beyond the colonial boundaries, and a few whites. After
its first establishment the line of policy adopted by Government was
judicious, and well calculated to promote the ultimate success of
the undertaking. Assistance was very sparingly afforded, and the
people were led to depend more on individual exertion than to expect
extraneous aid from whatever quarter. Due attention was, however,
paid to their moral improvement, and in the selection of a Minister
the choice has fallen upon an individual every way suitable."

"For some time after their arrival, the people had to struggle
with difficulties of no ordinary magnitude, and the circumstances
alone of their being placed in possession of a country where a
powerful tribe of Caffres had been just driven, under feelings exasperated to the highest pitch at their expulsion, and who did not
scruple to declare their fixed determination to obtain compensation
by reprisals on the Colonists, was in itself sufficient to depress the
ardour of the sanguine, and to deter the timid from placing themselves in a situation so extremely precarious. But notwithstanding
the repeated inroads of these people, the intrepidity displayed on
such occasions by the inhabitants of the Settlement, the rapidity
with which they pursued the depredators whenever cattle were
carried off, and their peculiar shrewdness in tracking them to the
kraal of the plunderer, have so successfully counteracted such
attacks that they are now shunned by their marauding neighbours ;
being a people whom it is not altogether prudent to meddle with."

"The stock they at present possess consists of 200 horses and
mares, 2,200 horned cattle, and 6,000 sheep and goats ; they
have also among them 35 bullock wagons."

The letter signed R. G. called forth an answer from "A
Farmer," in No. 27 of the *Journal*, 29th June, 1832, from
which the following is an extract :—

"It is (Kat River) a spot favoured by Nature beyond all other portions of the Colony, and appropriated, judging by what almost daily takes place, to the use of *all* such Hottentots as choose to resort thither ; no matter whence they come, under what circumstances they left the service of their employers, or how they got possession of the stock with which they came provided ; sojourners there enjoy a degree of freedom unknown to any of the civilized countries of Europe, they are exempt from the inconvenient control of a Resident Magistrate, and the place, taken all in all, is justly regarded by the idle, the profligate, and by delinquents of every magnitude, as the most perfect place of sanctuary which the whole globe affords."

This correspondence was continued for a considerable time between R. G., "A Farmer," and others. In replying to "A Farmer," R. G. (Mr. Godlonton) quotes a Government advertisement, dated January 11, 1832, which, however it may have been discredited at the time, proves the correctness of the adage, that "coming events cast their shadows before"—for twenty years afterwards, the very report described in the first paragraph of the Government advertisement actually took place, by a large portion of the coloured inhabitants of the Kat River going into rebellion, "aided by the Kafirs." The Proclamation appeared in the *Graham's Town Journal* of January 6, 1832 :—

"GOVERNMENT ADVERTISEMENT.

"Colonial Office, Cape Town.

"It is with much regret that His Excellency the Governor feels himself under the necessity of noticing thus publicly the prevalence of a report which has been, and still continues to be, circulated throughout a large portion of the Eastern Division of the Colony, to the effect that an Insurrection, *directed against the Colonists*, had broke out, or was on the point of breaking out, among the Hottentots located on the Kat River, *aided by the Kafirs*.

"The absurdity of this rumour became instantly apparent to the Local Authorities on the Eastern Frontier, who lost no time, however, in endeavouring to trace the probable causes of its origin ; and His Excellency has now the satisfaction to announce that no grounds whatever did, or do, exist for the invention and propagation of that most false and scandalous report.

"The Military Commandant and the Civil Commissioner, as well as the Magistrate of the Albany and Somerset Districts, were suffered to remain in ignorance of the apprehended danger ; whilst the rumour was circulated amongst the farmers with a very unusual degree of rapidity.

"Many of these, with some of the Field-cornets, took up arms, and almost the first intimation received by the inhabitants of Kat River of the danger to which they were exposed by the prevalence of the report, was the appearance of an armed party of farmers in their immediate neighbourhood.

"His Excellency has had occasion to feel, and has expressed his sense of, the value of the public services rendered heretofore by the inhabitants of the Eastern Districts of this Colony, when duly called out and acting with the troops in maintaining the peace of the Frontier, and repressing the turbulence of some of the tribes situated beyond its limits. It is, therefore, with great pain that he is now compelled to comment, in severe terms, on the culpable negligence of certain Field-cornets, who neither reported the alarm in the proper quarters, and at the proper time, nor, apparently, endeavoured to prevent proceedings which were not only contrary to law, but had a direct tendency to provoke and inflame the feelings of certain classes of the Colonists against each other.

"Those persons who have thus betrayed their readiness to put trust in absurd and most insidious reports,—to arm themselves against their fellow subjects,—and to risk the commencement of a state of things which would terminate in their own ruin, may rest assured that the Civil and Military Authorities are sufficiently powerful to repress any disturbances that might by possibility arise. Their united strength will be instantly put forth in crushing Insurrection wherever, and amongst whomsoever, it may show itself ; and His Excellency confidently anticipates that he will not again have occasion to mark his disapprobation of a line of conduct which he is inclined to believe arose rather from misinformation and prejudice, than from any deliberate intention to disturb the public tranquillity in a portion of the Colony which is happily advancing in improvement, founded on principles that promise fairly to secure its continuance.

" By order of His Excellency the Governor,

" (Signed) JOHN BELL,
" Secretary to Government."

The following year, in May, 1833, on returning from his next collecting tour through the Eastern Province, Mr. Godlonton wrote another of his interesting travelling sketches, which appeared in the *Graham's Town Journal* of the 16th May, 1833, under the signature of " A Traveller." It is here inserted to show that although in after years Mr. Godlonton disagreed with the late Sir Andreas Stockenstrom in politics, he did not withhold from that gentleman the acknowledged merit to which he was justly entitled. It will also be seen that over half a century has not much improved the morals of a large section of our Kafir neighbours :—

TRAVELLING SKETCHES.

Fort Beaufort, May 1, 1833.

To THE EDITOR : Sir,—In passing along the frontier from Cradock to the Southward, the traveller cannot but be struck with the great diversity he meets with both in the features of the scenery and the qualities of the soil and pasturage. For the first fifty miles, the country in general presents an appearance of great aridity, whilst the hills—some of them almost attaining the character of mountains, are scattered around in such profusion, and exhibit forms so grotesque and diversified, that it would puzzle a modern geometrician to find terms to describe them.

Immediately after crossing the Baviaans River, the country assumes a new aspect, and you enter upon a tract clothed with the richest pasturage, and adorned with patches of umbrageous thicket in a way that speaks more forcibly to the senses than all the eloquence of " *Burke* on the sublime and beautiful." A good road traverses the foot of a magnificent mountain range, the face of which, in many parts, abounds with timber of the finest description. On reaching the height which commands the splendid tract, granted to the Commissioner General, the honourable Capt. Stockenstrom, a thousand ideas will force themselves on the mind of any person accustomed to reflection. This meritorious officer has attained his high rank and his great popularity, by his incessant activity and his able arrangements in promoting the interests of the frontier, and particularly of that district over which he, for many years, presided as Landdrost (Graaff-Reinet), and it is certainly not improbable that the *oracular* distich composed by an Amateur Bard, one of his admirers, that

———Ages still to come,
Will hail the name of " patriot " Stockenstrom.

.   .   .   .

Behind the Kaga mountains is situated one of the Government forests, from whence the farmers of the Sneeuwberg and Graaff-Reinet districts procure their timber. There is another forest of equal extent, covering the face of the Kromme Range, a few miles only distant, and which contains woods of a similar description. In both of these are found trees of the most magnificent growth. Yellow wood of both varieties (*Taxus* and *Taxus elongatus*) is frequently found without a branch to the height of 40 feet, and at the butt six feet in diameter. Hard woods in request for wagon work, are likewise met with in great abundance and variety. The sawyers who inhabit these forests are principally emigrant-from the United Kingdom ; but the inhabitants of the neighbourshood complain, and I believe, with good reason, that they are the resort of and serve as a secure harbour to great numbers of idle and dissolute Hottentots, to whom they do not scruple to attribute many of the petty and vexatious depredations frequently committed upon them.

It was, perhaps, a lucky incident, that *Fortune* should, in one of her vagaries, transmit from the shores of *Scotia* to this part of the Colony, one of those enigmatical bipeds yclept a POET; the consequence is, that it has almost attained the rank and celebrity of classic ground. If the traveller have a spark of enthusiasm in his composition, a thousand fanciful images will be dancing through his mind, and sober realities will be presented in language refined and purified by the rarified atmosphere of the *Parnassian* Mount. Thus he finds as he proceeds, that he has "Kaga's dark mountains" behind him—the "cold and cloudy Winterberg" on his left hand,—that beneath this winds the "lone Mancanzana's margin grey," whilst on passing an execrable drift, he will be charmed to find that the stream which rolls over huge masses of loose rock, is no other than the "dark and rapid Koonap." On the height above this drift stands a deserted Military Post, which, together with the surrounding country to some extent, has, it is understood, been recently granted to the present Civil Commissioner of the Cape District.

This part of the Frontier being particularly exposed to *Caffer depredations*, the visitor will find he is compelled to listen to numerous tales of severe losses by these midnight plunderers. At the time I passed, one farmer had had 13 horses stolen; by immediate pursuit they were overtaken near the mouth of the Kat River, and though the robbers contrived to escape under cover of the thick bush the horses were recovered. Another person was informed by a boy that a party of Caffers had been seen driving his horses into a certain bush at no great distance from the house; on proceeding to the spot, the animals were found tied in the thicket for the purpose of being driven off when darkness should veil their proceedings. At another farm-house which I visited, a Caffer had been shot dead only a few days before my arrival. The farmer hearing about midnight an unusual noise among his sheep, supposed, as he stated, that a wolf had entered his kraal, and on proceeding with his gun to the spot, he distinguished a Caffer in the act of lifting a sheep over the enclosure: he instantly fired when the shot struck, not the robber in the kraal, but his com-

G

panion, who was crouched down on the outside for the purpose of receiving the plunder; on examin ing the spot, I found that the kraal was built to within the distance of two feet of the edge of a deep and rugged cavi ty, and it appears that the Caffer, when struck, fell headlong into this chasm and from thence rolled into a dry ravine below, where the body was found lying the next morning.

Such are the lamentable effects whic h are often recurring from the proximity of the frontier farmers to the Caffer Tribes, and perhaps, it will be quite impossible to adopt any method which will altogether put a stop to the depredations of these restless people. The existing system certainly requires amendment, and much might unquestionably be done in the way of improvement, were a proper understanding preserved with the Caffer Chiefs, but still it must be expected, that on an extensive line of frontier like this, which possesses so many local facilities for concealment and escape, depredations will occur even under the most perfect system ; and that, when the opposite parties come into collision, fatal results will occasionally follow. The military were very generally spoken of in terms of praise for the promptitude with which assistance was afforded in the depredations, and I heard of numerous instances, where timely notice had been given, in which stolen property had been retaken by the patroles ; but still it is very clear, that to give effect to the Colonial regulations and to maintain something like system, the Government must have accredited agents stationed in Cafferland, a measure that is alike required for the protection of the farmer and for the advancement of the frontier trade.

Along the whole of the route which I passed, the great Fish River is of so much importance to the inhabitants, that I cannot quit my subject without adverting to it. This stream may almost be considered at the *Nile* of this part of South Africa ; without it a great tract of country, in which are situated some of the finest and most fertile farms in this district, would be quite uninhabitable. Its extreme tortuosity is of immense advantage, as it thus gives fertility to a much greater extent of country than it would, were its course less impeded by natural obstacles. Innumerable streams pour their contents into this River, and the torrents which occasionally rush down from the mountainous country frequently augment its current,—more especially in the summer season when thunder storms are prevalent,—to the magnitude of a furious and impassable torrent. The quantity of matter which is rolled down into this river, and deposited at its mouth within a single year, must be immense. Its waters are not only greatly discoloured by it, but very frequently the sea where it disembogues itself, acquires the same yellow hue to a considerable distance from the shore. At such seasons it is altogether impassable, and as this is of very frequent occurrence it is a matter of surprise that among the other improvements on the frontier no measure has been adopted for constructing a bridge, or other means of preserving at all times a communication between one part of the district and another ; this is a subject of very great importance to the well being of the Frontier. There is, however, some reason to believe that the inconvenience will shortly be removed, as at one of the most frequented drifts an ingenious practical Mechanic has expressed his readiness to undertake to complete the requisite work for the small sum of £400, an expense that certainly cannot for a moment be set in competition with the imminent risk of life and property which frequently occurs when necessity compels the traveller to ford the river at hazardous seasons, or to the loss of time and great inconvenience which are often sustained by a detention on its bank for days together in tempestuous weather.

I am, &c.,

A Traveller.

The " City of the Settlers " having its own newspaper, also knew how to enjoy itself, as will be seen from the following account of a *Fancy Ball*, given by the Officers of H.M. 98th Regiment in the month of July, 1832:—

" Wonders never will cease ! Only think of a Fancy Ball in

Graham's Town! What would the old mimosa * say if it had been there. But a few years have passed since the founder of our town chose its shade for head-quarters." "I fancied the millenium commenced—the dwellers in all lands and the mighty dead of all ages were mingled—time and space were annihilated, and the lion and the lamb were sporting together. The renowned Beau Brummel led out, glittering in old Isaac's jewels, the representative of the lovely Rebecca; the deposed Dey of Algiers danced with good Queen Bess (who, by the way, somewhat anticipated the fashion by wearing a hoop), His Zulu Majesty, Dingaan, laid aside his assegai and shield, and footed it with a pretty Welsh peasant; a Malay Priest waltzed with a tight little Quaker, and the Imaum of Muscat flung the handkerchief alternately to little loves from Alp and Appenine, for whom he would apparently have exchanged all the joys of his fabled Paradise," &c., &c., "and I trudged home," says the writer, singing—

> Dance, Regan, dance, with Cordelia and Goneril,
>   Down the middle, up again, pousette and cross;
> Stop, Cordelia, do not tread upon her heel,
>   Regan feeds on coltsfoot and kicks like a horse.
> Round let us bound, for this is Punch's holiday,
>   Glory to Tomfoolery,—huzza, huzza.

The *Graham's Town Journal* continued to be conducted by the writer, with the assistance of the late Lieut. T. C. White, of Table Farm, until that lamented gentleman was killed by Kafirs at the Kei River in the war of 1834-35. The late Mr. W. Beddy, of Trinity College, Dublin, formerly editor of the *Colonist*, printed in Cape Town, was then engaged

---

° In the very centre of High-street stood for many years a *Mimosa Tree*, indigenous to the country, near which it was said Colonel Graham, the founder of Graham's Town, pitched his tent when the Zuurveld was cleared of Kafirs in 1819, and that in the stem of this tree he drove a nail, upon which he hung his sword. The tree, with the nail stuck in it, was afterwards protected by a wooden railing, round which were seats. The tree, by what means the writer is unaware, was eventually removed, as well as the railings.

by the proprietor, at a salary. In the beginning of 1834, the proprietor entered into an arrangement with Mr. Godlonton to edit the paper, and after a few months, induced the latter to leave the Government service, and join the proprietor in partnership for a term of five years, the proprietor finding the capital, and the printing establishment remaining his private property. The following Advertisement was then published in the *Graham's Town Journal* of July, 1834:—

NOTICE

Is hereby given, that the Business of *Printer, Bookseller, Stationer* and *Bookbinder*, hitherto conducted by L. H. Meurant, will, from this date, be carried on in the joint names of the Undersigned.

(Signed)   L. H. MEURANT.
R. GODLONTON.

Office of the *Graham's Town Journal*,
17th July, 1834.

In July, 1839, the partnership having ceased by effluxion of time, the writer sold the whole of the printing establishment, together with his share of the goodwill of the *Journal*, to his late partner, Mr. Godlonton, who thenceforth continued the *Journal* as his own private property. New iron presses and other improvements had been imported by the firm of Meurant & Godlonton, but the old historical *Wooden Press* was retained by Mr. Godlonton, as stated by him in the description of its importation and subsequent seizure.

Up to this period and long after the *Graham's Town Journal* continued to be the only newspaper published in the Eastern Province. On the 2nd April, 1845, the first number of the *Eastern Province Herald* was published at Port Elizabeth by Mr. John Ross Philip. The late Mr. John Paterson, M.L.A., then Government Schoolmaster at Port Elizabeth, assisted

Mr. Philip by writing for it. Mr. Paterson subsequently got out printing materials of his own, about the latter end of 1849, and started another paper, under the title of the *Eastern Province News*. The *Port Elizabeth Mercury* and *Port Elizabeth Telegraph* were started about the same time. Later on Mr. Paterson dropped the title of *News*, and by some private arrangement with Mr. Philip resumed the old name *Herald*. The *Eastern Province Herald* was the first newspaper issued in Port Elizabeth, and the second in the Eastern Province. The present talented editor, Mr. George Impey, bought the plant from Mr. Paterson in October, 1857, and has been the editor and proprietor, or co-proprietor, ever since.

The *Port Elizabeth Telegraph* was started by Mr. Henry Dunlop Dyke, and the *Port Elizabeth Mercury* by Mr. J. R. Philip, which latter paper was, however, afterwards discontinued. Mr. Dyke took over Mr. Philip's portion of the plant, but the paper was afterwards discontinued in consequence of the death of Mr. Dyke. The plant was then sold by auction and purchased by Messrs. Richards, Impey & Co., who again sold it to Mr. James Kemsley, who, from that time forward, published the *Port Elizabeth Telegraph*. Such is the history of the first newspapers established in the Eastern Province. The number has increased, including Natal, the Free State, Transvaal and Diamond Fields, to upwards of *one hundred and fifty*.

APPENDIX.

List of South African newspapers filed in the Colonial Office, Cape Town, up to the 1st day of February, 1881, when the list was prepared. It is, however, not so complete as might be wished :—

Agricultural News
Agricultural Register
Adelaide Standard
Albert Times
African Journal
Alice Times
Aliwal Observer
Aliwal North Standard
Anglo-African
Beaufort Courier
Bedford Advertiser
Boerenvriend
Burghersdorp Gazette
British Settler
Cape and Natal News
Cape Argus
Cape Frontier Times
Cape Mercantile Advertiser
Cape Mercury
Cape Town Mirror
Cape Town Mail
Cape Town News
Cape Standard
Cape Times

Cape of Good Hope Observer
Colonist (Cape Town)
Colonist
Colesberg Advertiser
Commercial Advertiser
Cradock News
Cradock Register
Daily News
Daily Times
Diamond Field
Diamond Field Advertiser
Diamond News
East London Dispatch
Echo
Eastern Star
Eastern Province Herald
Empire
European Mail
Evening Express
Evening Star
Examiner
Express (Orange Free State)
Eastern Province Mercantile
    Advertiser

East London Advertiser
Exchange Gazette
Fort Beaufort'Advocate
Friend of the Sovereignty
(O. F. S.)
Friend of the Free State
(O. F. S)
Frontier Guardian
George Advertiser
Germania
Graaff-Reinet Advertiser
Graaff-Reinet Courant
Graaff-Reinet Herald
Graham's Town Advertiser
Grensburger
Grocott's Penny Mail
Great Eastern
Guide
Graham's Town Journal
Independent
Kaffrarian Watchman
Kaapsche Grensblad
King William's Town Gazette
Lantern
Meditator
Middelburg Gazette
Mining Gazette
Mossel Bay Advertiser
Midland Province Banner
Natal Colonist
Natal Independent
Natal Mercury
Natal Witness
Northern Post
Observer
Oudtshoorn Courant

Overberg Courant
Observer
Patriot
Penny Post
Port Elizabeth Telegraph
Port Elizabeth Mercury
Queen's Town Free Press
Queen's Town Representative
Richmond Era
Sentinel and Meditator
Sentinel
Shipping and Commerical
Gazette
Sam Sly's African Journal
Shopkeeper's Journal
Somerset East Advertiser
South African
South African Com. Advertiser
South African Chronicle
South African Dominion
South African Mail
Standard and Mail
Statist
Tarkastad Chronicle
Tarkastad Herald
Times of Natal
Transvaal Argus (Transvaal)
Transvaal Advocate (do.)
Uitenhage Chronicle
Uitenhage Advertiser
Uitenhage Times
Verzamelaar
Victoria West Messenger
Volksblad
Volksvriend
Volksstem (Transvaal)

Ware Afrikaan	Worcester Weekly News
Weekly Chronicle	Worcestersche Courant
Weekly Magazine	Western Province Advertiser
Worcester Courant	Zuid-Afrikaan.

Several of the above papers have been discontinued, and others, not included in the above list, started ; but it will show the spread of newspaper literature in the Colony since the inestimable boon of the FREE PRESS was obtained.

The following letter was addressed by the writer of these " Reminiscences " to the Chairman and Members of the PRESS CONGRESS, held in Graham's Town on November 27, 1882 :—

Louisville, Riversdale, Nov. 18, 1882.

Messrs. RICHARDS, SLATER & Co.,
　　Proprietors of the *Journal*, Graham's Town.

Dear Sirs,—I have noticed with much satisfaction that it is intended to hold a Press Congress in Graham's Town, as being the birth-place of the Press in the Eastern Province. Having been accoucheur at the birth on the 30th September, 1830, when I brought to life the first Printing Press in the Eastern Province in Graham's Town, I hope I may be permitted to express my sympathy with the movement, and to bear my humble testimony, which I would have been glad to have done personally, to the invaluable services rendered to the Colony, but especially to the Eastern Province, through good report and evil report (for there was enough and to spare of the latter) by my dear and highly-esteemed old friend, the Hon'ble Robert Godlonton. I rejoice to know that he is alive, and that he will be able to be present at the Congress, and I hope will be further able to give the Inaugural Address. Editors, or Pressmen, as they are now called, have no idea now-a-days of what the labour of conducting and printing a newspaper was *fifty years ago*. Not only had my dear old friend to write leading articles, but we had to take off our coats and to print the papers ourselves, he "inking" the "formes," first with "balls," and afterwards with the improved "rollers," until our hands were blistered, once a-week, for a very considerable time. I regret very much I cannot be present, not only to add *one* to the number of "Pressmen," but to join in drinking the health of my dear old friend, Robert Godlonton, and prosperity to Graham's Town, a city in which I spent the best and happiest portion of my life, and which is as dear to me as ever.

Do not lose sight of the remarkable fact that the two proprietors of the *Journal* of *Fifty Years ago* are still alive, the one past four-score, and the other past three-score years and ten.

Please hand my hurried note to the Secretary of the Congress, and beg him to assure those present that the movement has my sincere sympathy.

Believe me, Dear Sirs,

Yours truly,

L. H. MEURANT.

To which the following reply was received :—

Graham's Town, December 8, 1882.

L. H. MEURANT, Esq., Riversdale.

Dear Sir,—I am directed to inform you that your letter, with reference to the Press Congress, was laid before the Press Union by Messrs. Richards, Slater & Co., and the reading of it was received with pleasure. The Congress ordered that it should be recorded and printed with the "Records of Proceedings," copy of which I will forward you when out of the Press, as I have done the "Press Union Constitution." The members of the Union exceedingly regretted that Mr. Godlonton and yourself were unable to be present.

I have the honour to be, Sir,

Yours obediently,

(Signed)   T. SHEFFIELD, Secretary.

It may not be uninteresting to note the market prices of Colonial produce in Graham's Town on the 30th December, 1831. The currency, which was then Rixdollars (1s. 6d.), Skillings (2¼d.) and Stivers (⅙th of a Skilling) being put into sterling:—

	£	s.	d.
Soap (Boer), per lb.	0	0	2½
Salt, per muid	0	6	2¼
Buck skins, each	0	1	0
Caffre hides, per 100 lbs. (dry)	1	10	0
Wet hides, each	0	10	0
Tiger skins	0	8	0
Bed feathers, per lb.	0	2	3
Onions, per muid	0	6	9
Tobacco (Boer)	0	1	2
Timber, per foot	0	0	2
Elephant Teeth, per lb.	0	1	9
Maize (Mealies), per muid	0	8	6
Meal (Cape), per muid	1	10	0
Wheat, per muid	1	0	0
Cheese (Albany), per lb.	0	0	3
Oats, per muid	0	4	6
Oathay, per 100 lbs.	0	2	0
Turkeys, each	0	5	0
Barley, per muid	0	4	0
Brandy, per half-aum	1	8	6
Butter (fresh), per lb.	0	0	9
Potatoes, per muid	0	3	0
Beans, do.	0	10	0
Peas, do.	0	10	0
Fowls, each	0	0	9
Ducks, do.	0	1	6
Horns, do.	0	0	6
Caffre Horns, per 100	2	2	0
Tallow, per lb.	0	0	2¼
Rush (water), per 100	0	4	0

Butchers' Meat, from ½d. to 1½d., per lb.